How to Build a Fire

. . .

How to
Build a
Fire

And Other Handy Things

Your Grandfather Knew

...

Erin Bried

Ballantine Books Trade Paperbacks · New York

A Ballantine Books Trade Paperback Original

Copyright © 2010 by Erin Bried
Illustrations copyright © 2010 by Simon M. Sullivan

Published in the United States by Ballantine Books,
an imprint of The Random House Publishing Group,
a division of Random House, Inc., New York.

BALLANTINE and colophon are registered trademarks of
The Random House Publishing Group,
a division of Random House, Inc., New York.

LIBRARY OF CONGRESS CATALOGING-IN-PUBLICATION DATA

Bried, Erin.
How to build a fire : and other handy things your grandfather knew /
Erin Bried.
p. cm.
ISBN 978-0-345-52509-3 (pbk.)—ISBN 978-0-345-52510-9 (ebook)
1. Men—Life skills guides.   I. Title.
HQ1090.B744   2010
646.70081—dc22   2010037682

Printed in the United States of America

www.ballantinebooks.com

2 4 6 8 9 7 5 3 1

Book design by Simon M. Sullivan

To Popi, Grandpa Norm,
Poppop, Grandpa B.,
and all grandfathers everywhere

Contents

· · ·

3 · Leading

4 · Prospering

5 · Thriving

6 · Bonding

7 · Playing

8 · Dressing

11 · Hosting

Introduction

. . .

"Every generation revolts against its fathers and makes friends with its grandfathers."
—Historian and philosopher LEWIS MUMFORD

I only knew one of my grandfathers, and though I loved him, I didn't know him very well. When my family managed to make the two-hour car trip to visit him, my older sister and I would greet him with hugs and kisses and then dash off to his two-tiered electric organ, where we'd plug in the giant headphones, bang away at the keys, and toy with the rumba beats until it was time to leave. When I think about my memories of him, only two really stand out: When I was little, he let me occasionally "shine" his bald head with a rag, and when I was in college he taught me to play a few chords on his guitar. In what I now realize was an act of supreme generosity, he even let me borrow his beloved Gibson so I could practice. I still have it. I still play it. And I still wonder what else he would've taught me, if only I'd asked.

The fact is, for whatever reason, many of us didn't ask (or even think of asking) our grandfathers about their lives. Maybe we were too young, or too timid, or even too arrogant, assuming we were smart and they were just, well, *old.* Since the days our grandfathers were born, we've invented television, the computer, the Internet, the iPod, the cell phone, the flu shot, hybrid cars, the GPS, and even the Large Hadron Collider. Heck, all of us were born in homes with electricity and indoor plumbing, and many of our grandfathers, as boys, were still finding their way by kerosene lamps and using outhouses. You'd think all of this progress would have made us a smarter, safer, more sustainable society. And yet we've somehow lost our way.

Think about it: With incredible thumb dexterity, we can make our video game avatars run, jump, punch, and shoot, but what do we really know about being brave in the face of danger? We email, chat, tweet, and share our status updates with the world at a frenzied pace, but would we even begin to know how to write a personal love letter? Would it even occur to us? We know how to program our iPods, but we don't know how to make our own music, or for that matter any of our own entertainment. We can memorize and repeat the talking points we hear on talk radio, but we've forgotten how to think critically and have our own big ideas. We take our civil rights for granted, but we often forget to be civil to one another. We hold opinions about who should win *Top Chef* and *The Bachelor*, and yet very few of us actually know how to catch a fish (much less cook one) or make a marriage last a lifetime. We buy fancy cars and drive them everywhere with absolutely no idea how to fix them if they break. We invest in big houses without knowing how to paint the walls or even, in some cases, clean the rooms. We, as a generation, are so proud of our accomplishments, our technology, our wealth, and yet we have absolutely no idea about half the stuff we're doing.

This is not sound footing. It's time to get back to basics and regain a sense of self-sufficiency before it's too late. And sometimes in order to move forward, you've got to look back. As members of the Greatest Generation, our grandfathers were defined not only by the Great Depression, but also by their heroic service to the country in World War II. Courageous, responsible, and involved, they understand sacrifice, hard work, and how to do whatever is necessary to take care of their loved ones. True, we've got Twitter down pat, but our grandfathers can teach us almost everything else we need to know.

I'm certainly not saying that all of us are completely inept in the grandfatherly arts. Take me, for example. Even though I never got a chance to *really* talk with my grandfather and I spend most of my time interviewing celebrities and writing profiles of them for my job at Condé Nast, I've managed to accomplish a few back-to-basics things I think would make him proud. After saving every penny for seven years, I bought my own apartment, a Brooklyn fixer-upper—which is a very nice way of saying a dump. I hung drywall, painted, installed molding, exposed brick, and made it a home. Because I love an ice-cold beer on a hot summer's day, I learned to brew my own (though sometimes with mixed results). I've spent the past five summers on Lake Erie fishing for walleye and, on the days when I get lucky, cooking them for dinner. I've managed to change two or three flat tires, though thankfully not all at the same time. Still, despite my efforts, I've only begun to scratch the surface of self-sufficiency, and there is a great deal I have yet to learn.

Because my own grandfathers are no longer alive, I reached out to ten others from all across the country to see what I could find out. The first lesson came quickly. When I called each of them and explained that I had written a book called *How to Sew a Button: And Other Nifty Things Your Grandmother Knew* and was now writing my second book, this one about grandfathers, they immediately asked how they could help. None of them asked how I found them. None of them questioned their own knowledge. They each literally did what they were called upon to do, and once I got them talking, they didn't stop.

"From the day I was born, whenever anybody asked me what I was going to do, I said, 'I'm going to be a pro ballplayer,' " Robert Kelly, eighty-two, told me. In 1948, at age twenty-one, he was signed by the Chicago Cubs, and over the course of his career he also pitched for the Cleveland Indians and Cincinnati Reds. "Boy, don't you think that was a thrill when I ended up playing for the Indians and standing in the middle of Cleveland Stadium against the Yankees? I took time to walk off the mound and look around the ballpark and gather it all in. It's still etched in my memory. The emotion I felt standing on the mound, facing Mickey Mantle. I was in awe!"

Charles Tatum, eighty-three, who was featured in the HBO miniseries *The Pacific*, had plenty of war stories. At seventeen, he enlisted in the marines, where he served under the leadership of famous war hero John Basilone, who won the Medal of Honor. They fought together in the battle of Iwo Jima, where Basilone was killed and Tatum, a machine gunner, earned a Bronze Star for his valor. I asked him how he found his courage. "We were trained to be soldiers. Everybody in war is afraid or scared, but I was different," he said, joking. "I was petrified." Then, more seriously, he explained how to be brave. "Even though you were scared, you were trained to do what you had to do. You didn't want to let your buddies down. You counted on them, and you knew they were counting on you. So, you had to put up."

Bill Holloman, eighty-five, cheekily told me the real reason why we won World War II. In 1942, when the U.S. military was still segregated, Holloman went to Tuskegee, Alabama, to train with other black soldiers to become a pilot. "I volunteered, because I thought I could affect the world. I thought my country needed me, and I was going to make the best darn pilot you'd ever seen." Fourteen months later, Holloman went to Italy, where he flew with the 332nd Fighter Group, or The Red Tails, whose members became known for their bravery and skill in escorting and protecting bombers on their missions. "After I completed my training, they told me to win the war. So I went over there, and I sent Hitler a telegram," he said, pulling my leg. "I told him I'd arrived and that he should surrender." When I asked him if Hitler ever wrote him back, Holloman laughed and replied, "No. But he listened to me, and then he quit."

Even prior to the war, many of our grandfathers, hard hit by the Great Depression, felt a sense of duty. "Times were tough," said Joe Toth, now eighty-seven, whose father worked in a steel mill. "We used to walk miles across railroad tracks and hills just to get to Father Baker's Orphanage, where we'd get one or two free loaves of bread. That'd help us out." Ever resourceful, he learned to help himself to other things, too. "The trains would come by loaded with coal, and we'd jump on top of them and throw the coal off. Later, we'd come back with a burlap sack, pick up the coal from the sides of the track, and bring it home. That's how we helped out."

Every grandfather has a story to share. Buck Buchanan, eighty-two, who grew up in Texas and later ran cotton-farming and shrimp-boating businesses, told me how he bounced back from the brink of failure. Angel Rodriguez, eighty-five, who immigrated from Colombia, told me how he found the wherewithal to work two jobs in a country where he couldn't even speak the language. Philip Spooner, eighty-eight, who was born on a potato farm in Maine, told me how he learned to fish at age two, chop wood at age six, and deliver a rousing speech at age eighty-six. Joe Babin, a ninety-three-year-old father of two, told me how to always stay coolheaded. Eighty-seven-year-old Al Sulka, who was married for forty-eight years before losing his beloved wife, told me how to have a long and happy marriage. Frank Walter, eighty-seven, who still hits the slopes every single day of the ski season, told me the secret to a long and happy life.

Before talking to these men, I knew that our grandfathers were brave, smart, and sometimes a bit puckish, if you caught them with that twinkle in their eye. But what I didn't know was how open they would be. Every single grandfather readily and eagerly shared his stories and advice, and to think, all I had to do was ask. Try it sometime. If you're lucky enough to have your own grandfather around, learn from him. Ask him big questions, like how he found the courage to go to war, and little ones, like how much cologne is too much. Ask him fun ones, like what was the first car he ever drove, and funny ones, like what's the best clean (and not-so-clean) joke he knows. Ask him when he hit his first homer, had his first cocktail, and fell in love for the first time. Ask him anything, really, and you'll find that if you take the time to sit and listen, the stories will just start pouring out. If you don't have your grandfather by your side, it's my hope that through this book, you'll have the spirit of him by your side, and you'll be smarter, happier, and braver for it.

Meet the Grandfathers

• • •

It's my great pleasure to introduce you to these ten incredible grandfathers, all of whom contributed their stories and wisdom to this book.

Joseph Babin

Joe Babin was born on September 27, 1916, in Cleveland, Ohio, where he had a carefree childhood. "The streets were our playground," he told me, adding that he and his friends played baseball and football just about every day. About a month after his thirteenth birthday, the stock market crashed, and his father's building supply business nearly went down with it. "It was touch and go, but there was always food on the table," said Babin, who attributed his family's ability to scrape by to his mother's frugality. "My mother was a good leader, so we managed." She budgeted so well, in fact, that Babin even had the opportunity to go to college and law school, a luxury some of his friends couldn't afford. "To get to high school, I'd walk two miles east from home," he said. "To get to college, I'd just walk two miles west." During his freshman year at Case Western Reserve University, he met his wife, Geraldine. "I needed a date for a fraternity dance, and my friend told me he had a girl for me. He used to chauffeur his mom around, and they made a call at my future wife's family home. He never even talked to her, but when we got home, he dialed her number and as soon as she got on the phone, he jammed the receiver in my face," said Babin, still incredulous after all these years. In case you're wondering, she said yes to the dance—and a few years later, also to marriage. A month after they tied the knot in 1941, the Japanese bombed Pearl Harbor, and two days later Babin was called up for the draft. He then enlisted in the air force and served as a groundling in North Africa, Sicily, and England.

Upon his return home in 1945, Babin went to work at his father's building supply business and embarked on what he considers his life's boldest undertaking: starting his own family. Now, whenever Babin drives around Cleveland—where he still lives—with his two children and four grandchildren, he can show them all the houses he helped build. Of all the things he helped raise in his life, though, it's the people in the backseat that make him proudest.

William Buchanan

Buck Buchanan, the youngest of the three Buchanan boys, was born on September 29, 1927, in McAllen, Texas. When the Great Depression hit, his father, a lawyer who'd invested heavily in real estate, went bankrupt, and though his mother held a job at the chamber of commerce, his family had to do whatever they could to get by. At first, they rented a small farm where they were able to grow their own food, and then the family moved to Oracle, Arizona, to mine for gold. "I can remember the dry creekbeds," said Buchanan, who attended a one-room schoolhouse there. Rather than striking gold, they struck out, and the family eventually moved to Rockport, Texas, where they operated a shrimping boat. Buchanan not only worked on the boat as a deckhand, but also helped build their house, which didn't have electricity or indoor plumbing, but did have an outdoor shower made of palm fronds. He spent his spare time at the beach. "We had a diving platform and raced tin boats," he told me. After he graduated from high school, Buchanan enlisted in the marines and spent the next eighteen months on an aircraft carrier in the South Pacific. "I was very, very fortunate," he said. "I got in after World War II and out right before the Korean War." In 1948, he enrolled in the University of Texas, where he met his wife, Sue. They married in 1951, and Buchanan left college to help his father grow and harvest alfalfa and cotton. While raising four daughters, he spent the next several decades farming cotton, operating heavy machinery for other farmers and oil field producers, and even building homes. Now, rather than watch his cotton grow, he enjoys watching his three grandchildren and four great-grandchildren grow. They're just as soft.

William Holloman III

On August 21, 1924, one of our nation's bravest pilots was born. All Bill Holloman ever wanted to do was to fly airplanes, but before he got off the ground, he spent plenty of time playing ball on vacant lots in his hometown of St. Louis, Missouri, and swimming, hunting, and camping on his grandparents' farm fifty miles outside the city. Because his father was a postal worker, his family managed to get through the Depression relatively unscathed, but Holloman's friends and neighbors weren't as lucky. "There were five of us in my family, but my mother *always* set a table for eight, and there were always eight people at the table. She'd let us bring some hungry kids home," he said. In 1942, Holloman enlisted in the still-segregated military and learned to fly at the Tuskegee Army Airfield in Alabama, where the first and only black pilots trained. During the war, he flew in the famed 332nd Fighter Group, The Red Tails, an elite all-black unit, which escorted and protected bombers on their missions. (Holloman recently consulted on the George Lucas film *The Red Tails*, starring Terrence Howard and Cuba Gooding Jr.) After the war, Holloman served as an instructor at Tuskegee, but before he had a chance to get a college degree he was ordered back into the air force to serve in the Korean War.

Despite spending years fighting evil abroad, Holloman still had to fight racism at home. Though he'd served in two wars, no American commercial airline would hire him because of his skin color, so he stayed in the military. "The color bar was still there," he told me. "I just wanted to do what I loved: fly airplanes." Eventually, a crop-dusting outfit in Central America hired him, and in 1957 a Canadian commercial airline offered him a job, after which he soon met his first wife and started his family. In 1966, he was recalled into service to fight in Vietnam, and by the time he returned to the States he'd found another mission: "When I came back, I became upset that most Americans didn't know that blacks flew in World War II." From that day forward, he dedicated his life to teaching history to younger generations, which include his six children, two stepchildren (he remarried in 1990), and seven grandchildren. It wasn't all lecturing, though. He also loved to travel with them—by air, of course. On June 11, 2010, a few weeks after my last interview with him, Holloman passed away, and the nation lost a hero.

Robert Kelly

From the day he was born on October 4, 1927, Bob Kelly knew he wanted to play baseball, which explains why he spent every free moment of his childhood in Cleveland, Ohio, at the sandlot. After he graduated from high school and put in a semester at Purdue, he was drafted into the army in 1946. "They put us on a train to Camp Atterbury, Indiana, where they gave us shots before they figured out where they'd send us. They wouldn't let us go to bed until we made our mind up whether we'd enlist or stay drafted. I got so tired that finally I said, 'All right, where do I sign?' " Kelly, who'd enlisted for eighteen months, went to Camp Lee in Virginia for basic training, and he stumbled across a baseball diamond where the camp team was playing. He joined the game and was soon offered a spot on the roster. "During the war, the navy and army teams were better than the major leagues, because all the guys were in the service," he said. In 1947, after he finished his military service, Kelly signed with the Chicago Cubs and played on their minor-league farm team. Soon after, he began dating his wife, Sandra, a high school classmate whom he'd admired but had previously been too shy to approach. Within three dates, he proposed, and within six months the two married. In May 1951, Kelly made his major-league debut, as the Cubs' pitcher, a position he'd hang on to until 1953, when he was traded to the Cincinnati Reds. He finished his baseball career in 1958 as a Cleveland Indian. After his retirement, Kelly opened a record shop. He then spent the next several decades working various sales jobs and raising his seven children. Now he lives with his wife in Connecticut, where he enjoys the occasional Manhattan cocktail. He also has fourteen athletic grandchildren and one great-grandchild, and he makes a point of cheering them on at as many of their games as he can.

Angel Rodriguez

Angel Rodriguez was born on a corn and yucca farm on November 28, 1924, in Palmar de Candelaria, a rural town in Colombia. He was the youngest of five children and son to a single mother. When he was three years old, his sister Paulina, who was thirty-two, traveled in search of work to the port city of Barranquilla, where she met and fell in love with a German optician named Adolf Kinderman, who immigrated to the country after World War I. As part of their marriage arrangement, Paulina insisted that she and Kinderman would raise her little brother Angel as their own, and he agreed. Rodriguez lived with them in Barranquilla, and almost immediately began to apprentice at Kinderman's optical shop. By age fourteen, he was able to run it on his own and did so for the next six years. Before long, political tensions in Colombia took their toll on Kinderman, and he lost the shop to another family, who kept Rodriguez employed. In 1952, after having a vision of an angel who told him to marry, he and his sweetheart, Gladys, tied the knot and expanded their family. In 1968, in order to give his children a better education, Rodriguez, who didn't speak any English, moved to West New York, just across the Hudson River from Manhattan, and got a job through a friend making glasses at the American Optical Society. "I had a good salary in Colombia, and I moved here and earned less. I used to cry, because I felt so stupid," he said. Still, he persevered, working hard at two full-time jobs and earning promotions, and in 1970 he was able to bring his wife and five children to America with him. They had one more child together, and in 1995 Rodriguez became a proud American citizen. Thanks to his dedication and handiwork, thousands of New Yorkers can now see clearly. Since his retirement, Rodriguez can often be found in Brooklyn at the home of his son, a Grammy-nominated jazz musician, where he and his large family, including thirteen grandchildren, love to boogie into the night.

Philip Spooner Sr.

Philip Spooner was born on a potato farm north of Caribou, Maine, on January 2, 1922. As a young boy, his chores included feeding the horses and milking thirty to forty cows at five o'clock every morning before school. He attended a one-room schoolhouse through the eighth grade, but since the nearest high school was twenty miles away (and his family didn't have a car), his education was cut short. Rather than continuing on, he became a janitor at his grade school, where his duties included lighting the stove and fetching water for a dollar and a half a month. At age eighteen, Spooner traveled north, ten miles shy of the Canadian border, to harvest lumber for thirty-five cents an hour. After that, he joined a road-building crew outside Bangor. "We lived in tents, and the boss's wife was the cook and I mean she really cooked: homemade pies and baked beans," he told me. Then he worked for a private contractor in the navy yard, and fell in love with a waitress named Jenny at a nearby restaurant, before being drafted for the war in November 1942. "It was love at first sight. We got married on Saturday night, and I left Monday morning for the army," he said of his late wife of fifty-four years. During the war Spooner became an ambulance driver and medic and saw action in all five major campaigns, participating in the Battle of the Bulge and the liberation of Paris. Not only did he carry injured soldiers to hospitals during battle, but he also transported Allied prisoners of war home from Poland, Yugoslavia, and Hungary and hundreds of injured Germans back to Germany. His unit earned the Presidential Citation. "I'm probably the only guy who sat with Eisenhower in France," he said. "He and a British big shot came to see how the bombing was going to go, so they put us ambulance drivers out back of the hospital tent, because we weren't all spruced up, and all we had to eat was K-rations. Eisenhower got out of the car and instead of going into the hospital and having chicken, he sat down in the grass with a K-ration and talked to us." After the war ended, Spooner returned to Maine, where he raised his four sons and one daughter and made a living driving trucks and delivering newspapers. In April 2009, Spooner, a lifelong Republican, made history once again when he made a speech to Maine's Judicial Committee. He said, "I am here today because of a conversation I had last June when I was voting. A woman at my polling place asked me, 'Do you believe in equality for gay and lesbian people?' I was pretty surprised to be asked a question like that. It made no sense to me. Finally I asked her, 'What do you think I fought for at Omaha Beach?' . . . For freedom and equality. These are the values that make America a great nation, one worth dying for." He's a hero not only to his two granddaughters and several great-grandchildren, but also to all those Americans who believe in equality for all people.

Al Sulka

Al Sulka, the son of Polish immigrants, was born on July 12, 1922, in Blue Island, Illinois, on the far South Side of Chicago. He spent much of his childhood playing basketball ("we had an old bushel basket nailed to a post in the alley") and, when he had the dime to spare, watching Roy Rogers westerns. During his summers, his father and mother—a railroad stevedore and a hotel maid—would send him, along with some of his six siblings, north to his uncle's farm in Michigan to pick strawberries and weed onions. In return, Sulka was paid ten cents an hour (which he promptly spent on school clothes) and his uncle would send his family sacks of potatoes, corn, and apples for the winter. Sulka also caddied at a local golf course. "I got fifty cents a round, and if you got a dime tip, then hallelujah! That meant you had a milk shake. It was tough during the Depression, but we pulled through." At seventeen, Sulka, along with his only brother, joined the Civilian Conservation Corps, one of the public works programs of the New Deal, and went to Oregon to build roads and fight brush fires. About three years later, in 1942, he enlisted in the navy, where he spent three of the next four years on the water off the coasts of Italy and Africa, repairing amphibious landing craft. He was lucky enough to be stationed in Staten Island on VE Day, May 8, 1945. "We had a three-day pass to go into Times Square, and I don't know if we slept those three days or not. You couldn't even move! Oh, we snake-danced. It was a big deal!" After the war ended, Sulka moved back to Illinois and in 1946 married his wife, Helen, whom he'd met at a town carnival just prior to enlisting. They had two children, and to support his family Sulka worked several jobs, including bartender, steel bender at a local factory, and even trash collector. Helen passed away in 1994. Now Sulka lives outside Chicago, in Crestwood, where he calls bingo (and breaks hearts) every Wednesday night, and entertains his three grandchildren and one great-grandchild with his very funny jokes. He has a lot of them.

Chuck Tatum

Though HBO's miniseries *The Pacific* drew upon his self-published book, *Red Blood, Black Sand*, about his experiences fighting in Iwo Jima, that's only part of Chuck Tatum's story. He was born on July 23, 1926, in Tulsa, Oklahoma. His father, an oil field builder, died of pneumonia when Tatum was just eight years old, and his mother, who later moved her brood to Stockton, California, raised all six kids single-handedly. Despite the hardship, Tatum recalls a happy childhood, shooting marbles, playing sandlot baseball, and collecting dime-store novels. "I became very interested in reading about airplanes and cowboys and crooks," he said. By age fifteen, Tatum, struck by a patriotic fervor, began begging his mother for permission to enlist in the marines. "I was afraid the war would be over before I could get in it," he said, adding that he selected the marines because "they had the best-looking uniforms." Eventually, she relented, and in July 1943 he went to Camp Pendleton in San Diego, where he trained as a machine gunner under Sergeant John Basilone, the famous war hero and Medal of Honor winner. The two fought side by side in the battle of Iwo Jima. In the thirty-six days it took to take the island, 6,821 marines, including Basilone, were killed, and more than 20,000 others were wounded. Tatum, then only eighteen years old, earned a Bronze Star for his heroism on the battlefield. In the summer of 1945, he returned to Stockton, where he became a fireman, married, had two children, and divorced. In the meantime, he decided to try his hand at car racing. "I found out that you could make good money. Some nights you could win fifty dollars! I wasn't making that in a *week*!" It turned out he had quite a talent for it, and eventually he designed and built his own race car, The Tatum Special, which was featured in the 1954 movie *Johnny Dark*. (Look closely, and you'll see Tatum driving the car.) By then, he'd also met and fallen in love with his second wife, Evelyn, whom he married in 1952 at age twenty-six. They had four children together, and in 1964, after a close call on the racetrack, Tatum, not wanting his children to grow up fatherless like he did, retired from racing and became a car salesman. Now he's looking forward to celebrating his sixtieth wedding anniversary. On the guest list: his eight grandchildren and three great-grandchildren.

Joseph Toth

Joe Toth was born in Buffalo, New York, on February 10, 1923. His father, like most in the area, worked at the steel plant as a bricklayer. "He had such hardworking hands. Every day he'd come home with blisters on his knuckles," said Toth. "When I saw those hands, I thought, *I'm never going to work in a steel mill*." With eleven siblings, everyone in the family had to chip in, and Toth remembered doing his part. "Everybody loved wearing knickers, because they had elastic below the knee. So, you'd go into somebody's yard with a fruit tree and pick fruit. Of course, you had holes in your pockets so you could fill your pockets *and* your knickers. By the time you were done, you'd be pretty heavy!" After graduating from high school, Toth attended Alfred University, a trade school, and worked on a government-run farm, milking cows and cleaning gutters. On Columbus Day, 1942, he enlisted in the navy and became a fire controlman (or ship gunner). Before he shipped out, one of his buddies introduced him to his fiancée, Frances. "It was love at first sight," said Toth. "I told my friend, 'If you screw up and lose Frances, she's mine!'" His friend did, and Toth soon won her heart. In the fall of 1943, he was scheduled to depart for the Pacific on the USS *Liscome Bay*, but the ship had too many fire controlmen, so everyone with last names beginning with *T* through *Z* got reassigned. After the ship departed without Toth, it took a direct torpedo hit by a Japanese submarine and sank, along with more than six hundred men aboard. "I just thank God my name starts with a *T*," Toth told me. When he got out of the service, he moved to Garfield, New Jersey, married Frances, and became an electrician. Together, they raised two children. Now he lives in Warwick, Pennsylvania, where his two granddaughters and four great-grandchildren visit him often. A navy man to this day, his grandchildren call him "Mate," and he loves to make their eyes light up by building them things, including giant dollhouses with hand-laid parquet floors, chandeliers, and tiny working light switches.

Frank Walter

On October 1, 1922, Frank Walter was born in Milton, Massachusetts, just outside Boston. His father worked for New England Bell Telephone, and after the stock market crashed, his mother picked up work with the Camp Fire Girls, a sister organization of the Boy Scouts. Life in the Walter household ran on a tight schedule: Supper was at 6 PM, bedtime was at 7 PM—and when he wasn't doing chores, Walter would roller-skate or play Ping-Pong with his two younger brothers. He attended Tufts University, but after his sophomore year, he enlisted in the navy with hopes of becoming a pilot. By March 1943, he'd earned his wings and soon after was selected to join the marines' Corsair Flying Fighter squadron in Okinawa. After the war ended, he remained in Japan as an operations officer. "I was the only captain who wasn't married, so I said I'd stay as long as I was needed," he said. In 1946, when he returned home, his parents threw him a party, where a childhood friend, Elinor, sat on his lap and asked him, "Well, Frank, are you going to marry me now?" He dodged the question.

After graduating from Tufts with a degree in mechanical engineering, Walter took a gig with the Chrysler Corporation in Detroit, which allowed him to work during the day and earn his master's degree at night on the company dime. He ended up working for the automaker for forty years, where one of his greatest achievements was conceptualizing the Plymouth Barracuda. "We conceived of it on the back of an envelope," he noted, adding that he also helped design the Fury and the Roadrunner. In the meantime, he'd married another woman, had one son, adopted a ten-year-old daughter, taken up skiing, and later divorced. In 1977, he sent Elinor a card out of the blue. She called him immediately, told him of her marriage, her four children, and her divorce. Almost exactly thirty-one years after her initial proposal, the two married. They shared eleven wonderful years together, often swishing down the slopes of Copper Mountain in Colorado, before Elinor lost her battle with cancer. Now he lives just off the lift line, as they dreamed of doing together, and he still feels close to her on the slopes. Maybe that's one reason he still skis every single day of the season, and as often as possible with his twelve grandchildren and six great-grandchildren.

1

Pioneering

. . .

Begin by knowing your way around your kingdom.
That way, you'll always be warm, safe, happy, and
well fed wherever you go.

Grow Up

• • •

*"Talk to plants, and they will grow. Life without love, for all living things,
is nothing. If you give love to something, it will reciprocate.
That's how we are as humans, too."*
—Angel Rodriguez

HOW TO PLANT A TREE

Step 1: Choose the right tree. Consider not only its size, speed of
growth, shape, and looks, but also its hardiness. It should be native to
your area and strong enough to weather the hottest and coldest tem-
peratures, and all the sunshine and rain you may or may not get. Other
things to think about: Will your tree lose its leaves every year (and do
you really want to rake them)? Does it bear fruit (and if so, will you eat
it or curse it when it's smushed on the bottom of your shoe)?

Step 2: Find a good spot. Look up, look down, look all around and
make sure your tree will have plenty of space to thrive. Your tree may
look small now, but it won't be for very long, and if you plant a soon-
to-be-big sucker right next to your house or directly under utility lines,
you'll be paying for that bad decision for years to come. Also, a no-
brainer: Before digging any holes, call your local utility company to
make sure you're clear of any underground cables.

Step 3: Dig a hole. A well-planted tree will grow faster and live
longer than a poorly planted tree, so take care to do it right. Using a
shovel, dig a big ol' bowl-shaped hole as deep as the tree's roots (or

root-ball) and at least twice as wide. The hole will most certainly look bigger than you think it needs to be, but the roots need that extra room to grow. Don't slack on the digging.

Step 4: Measure up. Place your tree in the hole and see if it's deep enough. If it's just right, proceed to step 5. If it's too deep, put some soil back. If it's too shallow, go have a lemonade. Then come back and keep digging.

Step 5: Position your tree. It should stand upright in the center of the hole. If your tree comes in a container, tap the pot to gently remove it, being careful not to rip the trunk from the roots. If your tree comes with its roots wrapped in burlap, plunk the whole thing in the pit and carefully remove the burlap, along with any twine, wire, nails, or staples.

Step 6: Fill the hole. Replace the soil you removed, packing it down firmly around the roots. You'll want your tree pit to catch water, so make sure your tree grows from the pit's deepest point. Then look for a little bulge at the base of your tree's trunk. It's called the root collar, and you want your soil to snuggle its bottom only. If you can't see your tree's collar, it may be planted too deep.

Step 7: Add water. Give the ground a good soak.

Step 8: Spread mulch (wood chips or bark) around your tree a couple of inches deep. It'll help keep the soil warm and moist, prevent weeds and erosion, and just make the whole thing look nice.

Step 9: Feel proud. Not only do trees help beautify the world, but they also help you save on energy costs, improve your water and air quality, give a home to songbirds, boost your property value, and fight global warming. Take good care of it by watering it once a week and pruning only dead or broken branches.

More Handy Tips:

- To find the best trees for your area, enter your zip code at Arbor Day.org and get all the information you've ever dreamed of. Better yet, join the Arbor Day Foundation for ten dollars, and you'll receive ten free trees of your choice. Seriously.

- If you're planting a sapling with naked roots, remove any packaging and soak the roots in a bucket of water for up to six hours before planting.

- If you're planting a tree that came in a pot and the roots look tangled once they're free, use a utility knife and make an X on the bottom of the root-ball and a vertical line down each side.

Aim True

• • •

"By the time I was six, I was splitting wood. Make sure you've got it lined up right and then go from there. It's not about muscle. The ax will do the work for you, but you can help it a little bit. If you're lucky, you'll hit it and have two pieces of wood. Usually, it takes a few blows. And don't cut your feet!"
—PHILIP SPOONER

HOW TO SPLIT FIREWOOD

Step 1: Dress appropriately. Wear safety goggles, leather work gloves, steel-toed boots, and a plaid flannel shirt, if you've got one. The first three items will help protect you from harm, while the last one will make you look butch. You'll also need a maul, which is basically a fatter version of an ax built specifically for splitting wood vertically, as opposed to chopping across it. (Axes will work, too, but because they're slimmer, they tend to get stuck in the wood more often, and that's just frustrating.)

Step 2: Set a twelve- to eighteen-inch log on end on a raised, flat wooden surface about fourteen inches tall. The perfect chopping block: a sawed-off tree stump. Your second-best option: on the soft ground. You may have to wrest your maul from the depths of the dirt sometimes, but that'll only help you build stronger muscles. Never ever split wood on pavement, or you and anybody in your vicinity will get hurt. Flying shards of steel? Not fun.

Step 3: Get in position, and eyeball where you'd like to split the wood. Cracks are nature's way of helping you along, so take advantage of them. Once you've focused on your target, place the sharp edge of your maul on it and, with your arms fully extended, grip the end of the handle with both hands. Step back a few inches so you're slightly reaching, and plant your feet shoulder-width apart.

Step 4: Prepare to strike. Pick up your maul and hold it parallel to the ground, across the front of your body, blade facing away from you. Place your weak hand at the base of the handle, palm facing down, and your dominant hand closer to the head, palm facing up. Grunt for good measure.

Step 5: Swing deep. Slightly bend your knees, and then raise your maul overhead with your arms extended, allowing your dominant hand to slide to the base of the handle. Keeping your eye on your target, swing your maul in a downward motion to meet the wood. Find the grace in the movement. Every woodsman knows that technique (and gravity) counts more than brute strength.

Step 6: Repeat as necessary. Maybe it'll take one good crack, maybe more. Just keep hitting your log in the same place until it splits. Then keep going until you have your desired amount of splits. Save the little pieces, too. They make great kindling.

Step 7: Stack 'em up and let 'em dry. If it's new wood, it'll be ready to burn in about nine months. If it's already seasoned, it's ready to burn now.

More Handy Tips

- Knotty, gnarly, or curvy wood can be tough to split. Save those pieces for last or, better yet, just use them for decoration.

- To gain more momentum in your swing, rise up on your toes before dropping your maul.

- If your maul does get stuck, keep a few steel wedges nearby and tap them into the wood with a little sledgehammer. That'll usually be enough to split the log into pieces and free your tool.

- Always remember, the best cure for a hot head and a cold house: splitting wood. Do it as often as necessary.

Stay Warm

• • •

"We used to go camping when I was a boy. We'd put a lean-to in our packs and head out and live off the country for three or four days. If you spend a night in the woods and you don't know how to build a fire, you're going to be cold."

—BILL HOLLOMAN

HOW TO BUILD A FIRE

Step 1: Find a good spot. Look for a clearing, one that's far away from houses, trees, roots, and overhanging branches and also sheltered from the wind. Then clear a circle about three feet across, brush or dig out the center so it's slightly concave, and place big, dry rocks around the edge.

Step 2: Gather your supplies: matches, tinder (twigs, dried grasses and leaves, newspaper, and so on), kindling (sticks smaller than your wrist), two or three dry, split, seasoned logs about twelve to eighteen inches long, and a pail of water (or sand or dirt) for safety.

Step 3: Build a tepee-shaped blaze. Just toss your tinder into the center, leaving space for oxygen to circulate around it. Stand your smallest pieces of kindling on end to form a pyramid over your tinder. Repeat with three or four larger pieces of kindling. Then, without knocking the whole thing over, hold your breath and very gently lean a couple of logs on top. Exhale.

Step 4: Strike a match, light your tinder, and watch it all go up in flames, just as you'd hoped. Once the fire really gets roaring, the logs will topple over the hot coals to keep burning. Add more logs as needed, being careful you don't smother the flames.

Step 5: Get out your s'more fixin's and let the ghost stories begin. Did you hear the one about the guy with a hook for a hand? What about the girl with the ribbon around her neck? Come to think of it, who is that standing behind that tree?

More Handy Tips

- If there's not a lot of tinder around, you might have to get creative. Try dried pine needles, pieces of papery birch bark, a fallen bird's nest (pulled apart), or even the fluff from a cattail (ahem, the kind that grows in wetlands, not the kind that is connected to your neighbor's kitty). Pine pitch (or sap) will always light, even on wet days. So will a cotton ball swabbed with Vaseline.

- To identify good fire logs, knock two together. If you hear a clunk, they're ready to burn. If you hear a thud, they're probably still too wet to do anything but smoke you out.

- Never build your fire on top of rocks, and never toss rocks into it, either. Hot rocks can explode, possibly causing harm to anyone nearby.

- Never leave an unattended fire burning. Always, *always* put it out, using water, sand, or dirt.

- To prevent your matches from getting wet, dip their tips in wax and store them in an empty film canister.

- No matches? Build a fire plow. Find a piece of soft wood about a foot or two long and a very hard, pointy stick, about a foot long. Rub the point of your stick along the grain of the soft wood until you form a groove. When you see saw dust collecting, rub faster; you'll eventually get a tiny burning ember. Touch it to your tinder, and ignite your blaze. It may not be the quickest way to start a fire, but it sure beats freezing your you-know-what off.

Stay Afloat

• • •

"We had tin boat races in the basin, and they were thrilling. You'd fold up a piece of corrugated iron, about three feet wide and eight feet long, and fasten it together on the ends with screws and tar. I had one that I called the Orchid, which I painted lavender. I was doing real well in the race, but then I got too exuberant and I capsized it and it sank. Of course, I swam down and brought it back up again!"
—Buck Buchanan

How to Paddle a Canoe

Step 1: Climb aboard. This is the hardest thing you'll do all day, but if you can get in a canoe without tipping it, then you'll be golden on the pond. Just stay low in a crouched position, step as close to the center-line as possible, and slide both hands along the sides to steady yourself as you walk toward your seat. If you're alone, sit in the back of the boat.

Step 2: Grab your paddle. If you're right-handed, grip the paddle with your left hand on top of the handle and your right hand on the shaft, closer to the blade. To check your grip, hold the paddle in front of you, parallel to the water. Your arms should be just slightly wider than shoulder-width apart.

Step 3: Use the simple J-stroke, so you don't have to be bothered switching sides with every paddle. While keeping your chin up and back straight, reach high with your paddle and then dive it into the water just ahead of your knees. The blade should be perpendicular to the boat and fully submerged. Then draw your paddle alongside the boat, and when your left hand is extended across your body and your right hand is even with your hips, turn the blade parallel to the boat and use it as a rudder; push it gently away from you to scoop out a gentle J-shaped hook. (On the right side of the boat, it's actually a backward J.) Repeat the stroke from the start.

Step 4: Check your course. If you're paddling properly, you should be going in a straight line.

More Handy Tips

- Always wear a life preserver and sunscreen when boating. Both can save your life.

- When your arm gets tired, switch sides (and grips), and use the J-stroke on the other side. Remember, your J should always hook away from the boat.

- Keep your boat straight in rapids and waves. If you approach either sideways, you'll swamp your boat, and it'll sink.

- If you plan on paddling for a long time, bring water with you. A snack couldn't hurt, either. And toss a change of clothes in a dry bag, in case you happen to get wet.

Get Hooked

* * *

"When I was two and a half years old, my grandfather got an alder limb, a piece of twine, and a fishhook. He put an angleworm on the hook and set me loose at the creek behind our house. I caught a trout about four inches long! I came back and showed my mother. She didn't know I was fishin'! She looked at my grandfather and said, 'You left him all alone?' My grandfather said, 'He's old enough to go fishin'. See? He caught one!'"

—PHILIP SPOONER

HOW TO CATCH A FRESHWATER FISH

Step 1: Gather your equipment: a spinning rod and reel (with hook, line, and sinker attached); some bait; an ice-filled cooler for your catch; a sandwich, drink, and chips (for you, not the fish); and your fishing license. (Get one at your local bait shop before you go, or you may be hit with a very large fine. What's worse, you won't get to keep your catch or possibly even your equipment.)

Step 2: Time your trip. Fish don't typically bite all day long, so you've got to know when to work your pole. Ask a local for advice, or follow these general rules: Cast in the afternoon in spring and fall. You've got to give the fish enough time to literally warm up before they get hungry. In summer, get out there in the wee hours of the morning, before breakfast. Missed your alarm? Try again at dusk.

Step 3: Find your spot. If you don't know the area, hit the local bait shop and start asking questions. If there's no one around, remember this: Fish, much like people, like food and shelter. In a lake or pond, that means they're likely to hang around rocks, weeds, holes, inlets, piers, and underwater shelves. In a river or stream, you'll likely find them in deep pools or eddies, at the bottom of waterfalls, under drooping tree branches, beneath waves, or near rocks. Basically, you know, anywhere.

Step 4: Bait your hook. Thankfully, most freshwater fish will eat worms, which industrious fisherman can score for free. (Just venture into your backyard at night after a good rain with a shovel and flashlight, and you'll be set. Once you dig some up, keep your worms in a dirt-filled box, punched with airholes, so they can live and breathe until they're ready to swim.) Open your box, select your worm, and size it up. If it's giant, break it into two pieces and return one half to the box. Then press your hook through the tip of your worm; repeat once more so your worm is doubly pierced and the end of your wriggler dangles from the hook.

Step 5: Cast your line. Holding your rod in, say, your right hand, allow your lure to hang about ten inches below the tip and then hook the line with your right index finger just in front of the reel. Use your left hand to flip open the bail—the metal guard that sits atop the line on your reel. Then, keeping your elbow close to your side, draw the tip of your rod back either over your shoulder or, if there are trees overhead or people behind you, out to your right side. With a snap of your wrist, propel your rod forward as you release your index finger from the line. When your worm takes a dunk or gets to your desired depth (you can tell by how much line you've let out), turn the handle on your reel to close the bail.

Step 6: Work your pole. Don't just sit there and daydream, or you'll never be able to feel when you've got a fish on the line. Slowly pull the tip of your pole against the current and reel in your line by a crank or two, and then repeat, until you've brought your lure all the way in. Then cast again.

Step 7: Set your hook. When you see the tip of your pole bounce or you feel weight on the end of it, chances are an unlucky fish has taken your bait. Jerk the tip of your pole upward to sink the hook in his lip. If you missed it, open your bail right away and let your line out a bit, so you can try to catch one of his friends in the same area. If you don't feel another hit soon, reel in to make sure the fish didn't steal your worm.

Step 8: Reel him in. Once you've got a fish on the line, bring him in slowly and steadily. If it's a monster, however, you may want to let him run a bit to tire him out, before you bring him in. Keep your rod tip up and tension on the line the entire time, or you risk losing your catch.

Step 9: Net your fish, especially if he's a big one. Once your swimmer is within reach, dunk your net into the water (or better yet, have a friend do it) and lead your fish into the net headfirst. Then scoop him up. Never pull a big fish out of the water, or he may free himself by either jumping off your hook or breaking your line.

Step 10: Grab your fish. Once you've got your fish on shore or in your boat, take a moment to give thanks to him for giving you his life. Then get a good hold of him. If he doesn't have sharp teeth or spiked fins, you can most likely grab him around the belly or by his bottom jaw. If he's got a good set of chompers, you can pick him up by sliding your fingers under his gills.

Step 11: Remove the hook. Grab the hook at its base and gently back it out, taking care that the barbed tip doesn't harm the fish. Use needle-nose pliers if the hook is deep or dangerously close to sharp teeth.

Step 12: See if he measures up. Hold your fish to a ruler (there's usually one built into your tackle box) to see if he meets the minimum size limits. If he does, hooray for you. Toss him into your cooler, and then call home to let everyone know what's for dinner. If he's too small, toss him back into the water and let him grow. Maybe you can catch him again next year.

More Handy Tips

- Every fisherman has an opinion on what it takes to be successful, but there is only one tried-and-true method. The secret to catching a lot of fish? You've got to fish a lot. That's it.

- When casting, remember that it's more of a flick than a throw. Finesse will get your line much farther than muscle.

- If you have a hard time gripping your fish once you land him, try wrapping an old towel around him and then picking him up. It'll protect your hands from any spikes, and make the fish less slippery.

- For more fishing tips and tricks, visit takemefishing.org.

Get Roped

· · ·

"The bowline is a knot you can trust. You pull it and it just gets tighter!"
—Joe Toth

How to Tie a Bowline Knot

Step 1: Eyeball where you'd like your knot. The bowline makes a big, no-slip loop at the end of a rope, perfect for, say, tying a boat to a pier or a tire swing to a tree. If you're not sure how big you'd like your loop, start two feet from the loose end of your rope. Make sure the loose end of the rope is on your right, and the long end is on your left.

Step 2: Make a rabbit hole. Flip the loose end of the rope *over* the long end of the rope to make a tiny loop, and hold that loop still by pinching it between your left forefinger and thumb. The tail, or loose end of the rope, should be dangling on your right side. Let's call that your rabbit.

Step 3: Run the rabbit. Using your right hand, pass the rabbit (aka the very tip of the loose end of the rope, not the whole thing) *up* through your rabbit hole, *under* and around the tree (aka the long side of the rope), and then back *down* through the rabbit hole.

Step 4: Tighten your knot by gripping the rabbit along with the nearest side of the resulting large loop in one hand and the long end of the rope in the other. Pull in opposite directions. Booyah!

More Handy Tips

- This knot's a tricky one to pronounce. To say it properly, unleash your inner hick and say the word *bowling*. Did you drop the *g*? If so, you're pronouncin' it perfectly.

- To adjust your knot, pull the slack in either direction and tighten.

- To untie a bowline, just fold the loop forward; it'll magically loosen.

- Practice tying this knot on its own and also around an object, like a tree or even your own hips.

Know Your Kingdom

· · ·

"You learn how to look down at the ground in the woods. Even pigeons leave tracks. You've got to know how to read the clues. If you don't know how to read the clues, you won't get the message."
—Bill Holloman

How to Read Animal Tracks

Step 1: Open your eyes. Unless you're looking for prehistoric fossilized tracks, you're not going to find very many clues on rocks (or rock-hard surfaces). The softer the ground, the better the track. You're golden if you happen to be on a riverbank, a muddy trail, a sand dune, or a snowy path.

Step 2: Use your head. Before you start the real detective work, consider which animals you know or suspect live nearby. For example, unless you live on the tundra, those big footprints in your backyard will more likely belong to your neighbor's dog than a grizzly bear. While you're at it, keep your eyes peeled for other contextual clues. Look for nearby habitats (nests, dams, dens, et cetera), fur, and feathers, as well as any other signs of life, like, well, you know, poop.

Step 3: Study the footprints. If the tracks have crisp edges, they're fresh. If the edges are worn or crumbled, or if there is debris in the tracks, they're old. Take note of the length, width, and depth to get an idea of the animal's size. Determine whether the animal has two or four feet, and check the distance between the strides to help understand his speed. (The farther apart, the faster he was going.) Finally, count the toes on each foot, and look closely for claw marks to help identify what kind of beastie passed through and which way he was going.

Common tracks (in ascending order, based on the number of toes):

Deer (two toes): Look for an upside-down heart, about two to three inches long, with a line between each half. Other possibilities: moose, elk. Appropriate reaction if you spot the animal: Get out your camera.

Mountain lion (four toes): Count four toes on each print, plus a heel pad with two lobes on the front edge and three on the back edge. Tracks will be about three to four inches wide, and the front paws will be larger than the rear. Retractable claws mean no nail marks will be visible. Other possibilities: bobcat. Appropriate reaction if you spot the animal (well after he's spotted you): Freak out on him. More specifically, make yourself bigger and louder than ever before until he (hopefully) runs away.

Coyote (four toes): You'll see four toes on each paw, often with claws, with the center two toes in alignment and the outer two toes almost triangular. The front paws are larger than the rear ones. The heel pad of the front paw has one lobe on the front edge and two on the back. The heel pad of the rear paw looks like a slightly smushed version. Coyote tracks are generally larger than dog tracks, and their paw prints run in a straighter line. Other possibilities: dog. Appropriate reaction if you spot the animal: Either scare him away, or give him a biscuit, but only if it's Fido from next door.

Squirrel (four toes in front, five in back): All rodents have four toes on their front feet and five on their back. Squirrels bound, which means their larger back feet land in front of their front feet. Other possibilities: mouse, chipmunk, porcupine. Appropriate reaction if you spot the animal: Meh, you see those everywhere.

Raccoon (five toes): Usually about two to three inches long, the raccoon track looks like a creepy, bony hand from a *Tales from the Crypt* episode with five long toes on each paw. The hind paws are longer than the front, and when the animal walks, you'll see the left hind paw next to the right front paw. Other possibilities: weasel, badger, otter, beaver, opossum, and skunk. Appropriate reaction if you spot the animal: Run home immediately. You're out way past your curfew.

Rabbit (five toes): Because rabbits hop, you'll find tracks from their oblong-shaped rear paws far in front of the tracks from their tiny front paws. Unlike squirrels, their front paws will be staggered, not side by side. Appropriate reaction if you spot the animal: Awwww.

Black bear (five toes): About three to five inches wide. You'll see five toes, each with individual claws, on each paw. The heel pad of the front foot looks similar to the ball of a human foot, only much larger. The heel pad of the hind foot will be about seven inches long, and it's triangle-shaped, almost like a massive piece of candy corn. (Mmm, candy corn.) Appropriate reaction if you spot the animal: If he doesn't see you, thank your lucky stars and back away slowly. If he does, wave your arms and talk to him in a firm voice. Once you get home, regale your friends with your tale of bravery—after you change your underwear.

More Handy Tips

- Carry a field guide with you when you're tracking animals to help you identify them.

- Don't forget your compass, in case you get lost.

- Remember that the tracks are not always perfect. In some ground conditions, only four toes of a five-toed animal may show up. Always remember to look for contextual clues.

2

Fixing

. . .

With a good set of tools and a little elbow grease,
you can make a happier home.

Get Screwed

. . .

*"You've got to have a halfway decent hammer, not too heavy, not too light.
It should do the work for you."*
—JOE TOTH

HOW TO ASSEMBLE A GOOD TOOL KIT

Step 1: Buy the basics, and don't cheap out, either. Good, quality tools will not only get the job done more quickly and safely, but they'll also last you a lifetime, saving you money in the long run. Plus, they'll make you look like you know what you're doing. Invest in:

- A hammer: A sixteen-ouncer will drive any nail. Old-school wooden handles are fine, but fiberglass or graphite handles absorb the shock better. Make sure it has a curved claw on its rear end, too, so you can remove old or wonky nails.

- Two screwdrivers: You'll need a four-pointed Phillips-head screwdriver and a flathead screwdriver. Higher quality usually means a harder tip, which helps prevent bending, chipping, or breaking. If you can splurge, get two of each, with different head sizes.

- Two pairs of pliers: Pick up a pair of adjustable pliers that won't slip when you grip, and a set of needle-nose with rubber-coated handles for added safety.

- A measuring tape: Get a long, fat one—twenty-five feet by one inch thick. That way, if you have to measure something big, it won't go limp. Plus, it'll look cooler, hanging from your belt. You know what they say about a person with a big measuring tape? Good measurer.

- A utility knife: Nab a metal one with replaceable blades, not a plastic one, or it'll surely crack.

- A level: A two-footer will set you straight.

- A handsaw: A fourteen-inch handsaw will probably fit in your box, and it'll be sturdy enough to make any necessary cuts. If you prefer to go high-tech, pick up a circular saw.

- Fasteners: Pick up a good assortment of screws, nails, and anchors—and if you plan on hanging pictures, some hooks and wire.

- A stud finder: It'll make hanging things much easier.

Step 2: Invest in safety gear. Now, don't just roll your eyes at this one, or you may not have two eyes to roll for long. Always wear goggles to protect your peepers. One sliver of a split nail can do more damage than you can probably imagine. Also, pick up a decent pair of leather work gloves to protect your hands and keep them soft. (You may not care about that last part now, but someday your sweetie will.) If you plan on sanding things, invest in a dust mask as well.

Step 3: Box them up. Get a good metal box with a sturdy clasp. When in doubt, choose red. You'll never lose it, and you'll look good carrying it, too.

More Handy Tips

- Good tools last forever. If they're too expensive at your local hardware store, consider picking them up at a local flea market. You can usually find some great deals there.

- Got a little extra to spend? Invest in a cordless drill, and a set of drill bits, too.

- Be generous with your tools. If a friend or neighbor asks to borrow one, allow it. And if you need to borrow a tool from someone else, just be sure to return it as soon as you finish the task at hand.

Get Hammered

• • •

"You always had to have a couple of nails in your pocket and a hammer handy."
—PHILIP SPOONER

HOW TO DRIVE A NAIL

Step 1: Place your nail. Pinching the shaft of the nail between the forefinger and thumb of your weaker hand, hold it in where you'd like it to go and at the angle you'd like to drive it.

Step 2: Set your nail. Choke up on your hammer, holding it about halfway up the handle, and then gently tap the nail into place. Once it sticks, remove your hand from the nail. You don't want to leave your fingers in the danger zone for any longer than you have to.

Step 3: Finish the job. To get the maximum leverage, move your grip down the handle of your hammer until your hand is just a couple of inches from its base. Then, using your wrist and elbow, not your shoulder, swing your hammer to drive the nail. The fewer the strokes, the better you've done (and the less sore you'll be tomorrow). When your nail is flush with the surface, you're finished!

More Handy Tips

- Always watch your nail, not your hammer, or you'll end up with a smushed thumb.

- If you whack your thumb, bite your lip, wag your hand vigorously, utter a few choice words (if you're alone), and then try it again. Only this time, you know, aim better.

Make Room

...

"I believe in being patient. I don't rush. There's a wrong way and a right way, and I'm doing it the right way."
—JOE TOTH

HOW TO HANG DRYWALL

Step 1: Gather your supplies. You'll need loads of stuff, so get ready: drywall, drywall tape, joint compound, metal corner beads, a level, shims, a drill, drywall screws, a five-inch-wide knife, a ten-inch-wide knife, a pole sander, sandpaper of various grits, and the phone number of your favorite pizza shop.

Step 2: Check your studs. Hold a level or straightedge across the face of your studs to make sure they're all standing even. Shim any low spots, and shave or sand any high spots. It's a drag, but it'll be well worth it in the long run.

Step 3: Place your drywall. Starting at the lower left-hand corner of the wall, fit your drywall horizontally against the studs. The bottom edge of the board should be flush with your floor, and the right edge of your board should end in the middle of a stud. If your drywall doesn't end in the middle of a stud, you'll have to cut it, but don't worry. It's no big wup. To do so, just measure the length of the wall from the corner to the stud's center. Mark that length on the face of your drywall, and draw a cut line. Then lay a straightedge along that line and score your drywall, using a utility knife. Be gentle; you don't have to muscle it. Next, stand your board on end and snap it from behind. Sometimes a little knock of the knee does the trick. Using your utility knife, cut the paper on the back of the board. All done, and ready to go!

Step 4: Screw it in. Using a drill, fasten your drywall screws through the drywall and into the center stud at twelve-inch intervals. Then work your way out, driving in screws every twelve inches on every stud.

Step 5: Work horizontally. Continue across the bottom of your wall, fitting your drywall side by side until you've come full circle. Remember, each piece of drywall should begin and end midway on a stud.

Step 6: Start a second row, making sure you stagger the seams to help hide the joints and strengthen the wall. Repeat until your entire wall is covered. Then order a pizza and chill. You can deal with the seams tomorrow.

Step 7: Fill the joints. Now you're going to smooth your walls so the seams are imperceptible. Using a five-inch knife, spread a thin layer of joint compound into each seam and over each screw hole, scraping off any excess.

Step 8: Tape the joints. While the compound is still wet, unroll an arm's length of drywall tape, center it over the seam, and press it down so it's smooth. Run the tape to the end of the board, hold your knife perpendicularly against it, and rip the tape. Finally, smooth the tape with your knife, working your way from the center out and removing any excess mud.

Step 9: Tape the inside corners. Cut a piece of tape the length of the corner, fold it in half lengthwise, and press it into the compound you've already spread into the corner. Smooth out the tape, using your knife.

Step 10: Bead the outside corners. Attach a piece of metal corner bead on every outside corner, where two pieces of drywall meet, using drywall screws. Smooth compound over the bead. Let it dry overnight.

Step 11: Sand all of your joints, using a pole sander affixed with 120-grit sandpaper. Wear a mask while you do this, because it's dusty work.

Step 12: Apply more joint compound, this time using a ten-inch knife. Be sure to fill in any indentations, and then let it dry overnight. Sand with 120-grit paper. Have patience, and repeat once more: Feather the compound, let it dry, and this time sand with ultrafine, 200-grit paper.

Step 13: Go pick out some cool paint colors. You're ready to paint!

More Handy Tips

- If you've got a naked ceiling, too, hang your drywall up there first. Do the walls second.

- Mark the location of your studs when you put up the first row to avoid guesswork later on.

- Stop screwing when your drywall ever-so-slightly dimples. If you screw too deeply, you'll rip the paper and crush your wall. If you screw too lightly, you'll see every screw, even through the paint.

- If you're hanging drywall around a window or door, stagger your seams so they don't end at the edge of either fixture. Otherwise, your walls will be weak.

- You'll know your joint compound is dry when it turns white. Gray compound means it's still wet. Red compound means you got some pizza sauce in there. Try to be a little more careful.

- If you're hanging drywall over an electrical outlet, measure the distance to the outlet, its height and width, and cut it out of your board, using a utility knife or a drywall knife, before you hang it.

Make Your Mark

• • •

"Painting isn't hard. Before when you had the brush, it was rough, but not now with the roller. I painted a room in three hours. The hardware store will mix any paint the color you want. They've got so many colors, it's ridiculous. Naturally, they'll want to sell you the best, but you don't really need it."

—AL SULKA

HOW TO PAINT A ROOM

Step 1: Prep your space. Remove all curtains and blinds, switch covers, and electrical plates, and move out as much furniture as you can. The emptier your room, the easier it is to paint. If you can't clear it entirely, move whatever's left to the center of the room and cover it, and all your floors, with tarp, taped down at the edges with painter's tape. Also, apply tape to the edges of any woodwork, windows, or doors you'd like to protect.

Step 2: Scrub your walls, using warm, soapy water. Rinse them with a damp towel, then allow them to dry.

Step 3: Make repairs. Fill any dings or dents with joint compound or spackle and a putty knife; let this dry. Then sand and wipe clean with a damp sponge. Fill any gaps along the ceiling, floor, or molding with painter's caulk. Smooth with a damp finger.

Step 4: Prepare to paint. Invest in decent paint, opting for one with low or, even better, no volatile organic compounds (VOCs). It's better for you and the environment. You'll need about a gallon for every 350 square feet of wall space. Also, gather any other supplies: a roller, a roller extension, two- to three-inch angled brushes, a paint tray, a few rags, and a ladder. Then pop your paint can and give it a good stir.

Step 5: Cut in at the edges. Because your roller can't fit everywhere, dip your small angled paintbrush into your paint and very carefully run it along the edges of your room and in the corners. Give yourself a good three-inch bumper.

Step 6: Roll it on. Carefully pour some paint into your rolling tray, coat your roller, and run it over the tray's grates several times to even out the paint. Then crisscross your roller over the wall. (Imagine painting a V or W, and then crossing it out with vertical lines.) Let it dry, being sure to cover your paint cans and wash out your brushes with warm soapy water. (Use a solvent if you're using oil-based paints.)

Step 7: Add a second coat, revel in your handiwork, and move your stuff back in.

More Handy Tips

- Prime your walls before painting if they're new or you're going from a darker color to a lighter one.

- Always paint from high to low, since gravity causes any paint splatters to fall. Start with the ceiling and work your way down.

- Canvas tarps work better than plastic ones, because they're heavier and absorbent. They're also more ecological.

- Never paint directly from the can. Always pour it into a cup or tray, so you don't spoil your mother batch with dust or brush hairs.

- When choosing your paint color, get free chips at the hardware store and tape them to your wall. Look at them in the daylight and at night, because the color will change in different lighting. The larger the wall, the darker the paint will look.

- To make a small space feel more open, choose lighter, cooler colors, like blues and greens, and paint the ceiling a shade of white to make it look higher. Sunset colors, like red, yellow, and orange, are like hugs. They make you feel cozy.

- The higher-gloss paint you use, the easier your walls will be to clean. Still, unless you're painting a soon-to-be-greasy burger joint, skip the high-gloss paint; it's just too darn shiny. Instead, use semi-gloss; it's perfect for doors and windows and in kitchens and bathrooms. Try eggshell or satin finishes on everything else to give your walls a warm, velvety quality. Be wary of flat paint; the low-gloss factor means you'll probably have to add another coat whenever you see any marks, stains, or imperfections.

Get Naked

. . .

*"My wife bought a piano at the Salvation Army. I had to strip off all the old
stuff on there. Strip, scrape, strip, scrape. It took me a long time to get it
down to the wood, but I'm quite proud to look at it now and say I did it. I get
such a great joy out of it."*
—BOB KELLY

HOW TO STRIP WOODEN FURNITURE

Step 1: Check the value of your piece. Did you buy it at the Salvation Army or a neighbor's garage sale for less than the cost of a pizza? If so, proceed to step 2. If you inherited it from your great-grandfather or you have a hunch that it may have once belonged to a king, queen, or famous dead writer, consult with an antiques specialist before you go at it with your scraper.

Step 2: Remove any hardware. If it's got knobs, take 'em off. And if anything is loose, jiggly, squeaky, or wobbly, fix it up by tightening the screws or adding some glue.

Step 3: Pick up a stripper. Um, yeah, not *that* kind of stripper. Get your mind out of the gutter, naughty pants. Buy a paint stripper, preferably an eco-friendly kind. Go for a gel or semi-paste version, which, you'll find, will very nicely cling to all the surfaces, even vertical ones. While you're at the hardware store, also pick up a cheapo natural-bristle brush to paint it on with, and if you don't have it already, get a putty scraper, some steel wool, fine sandpaper, and a tack cloth.

Also, maybe pick up a Mr. Goodbar. Who knows? You might need a snack later.

Step 4: Suit up. Hopefully you've bought an eco-friendly kind, but in case you didn't, know that stripper is seriously nasty stuff. Either way, put on some rubber gloves, an apron, and goggles; if you're not working outside, open all your windows. Place several layers of newspaper on the ground, beneath your furniture. While you're at it, vow to make a donation to an environmental group or cancer charity.

Step 5: Slap it on. Using your brush, paint on the stripper in a small area, and let it sit for the recommended amount of time, usually about fifteen minutes.

Step 6: Scrape it off. Now the fun part: Holding your putty knife at a forty-five-degree angle to the wood, gently push your scraper forward, along the grain of the wood, removing the stripper and any old paint or finish beneath it. If the finish doesn't come right off, don't muscle it or you'll scratch your furniture. Repeat until your wood is totally naked. Address any particularly stubborn spots with steel wool.

Step 7: Clean it. Depending on what kind of stripper you used, you may have to do something special to get any lingering bits off your wood. Check the stripper's instructions. Some will tell you to rinse it with water, while others will tell you to use something a little stronger, like turpentine.

Step 8: Sand it. Once all the paint is off, smooth the wood, using 120-grit sandpaper, then 220-grit. Have patience. This step feels the least satisfying in the moment, but makes the biggest difference in the end. Now remove any dust with a tack cloth.

Step 9: Finish it. Stain your wood, if you'd like; either way, apply a protective top coat of polyurethane, shellac, or tung or linseed oil. If you bought the piece from your neighbor, now's the time to offer to sell it back to him for double the price. Better yet, offer him a drink and thank him for the lovely piece.

More Handy Tips

- You'll know it's time to start scraping when the paint beneath your stripper loses its luster. You'll be tempted to go at it sooner, but don't do it, or you'll only create more work for yourself in the long run.

- Dull the corners of your putty knife before using it, or you may scratch your wood. Just drag it on a metal file or across some heavy-duty sandpaper. If all else fails, try dragging it on the side-walk.

- Have an old rag or towel handy so you can clean your scraper of gunk when necessary.

Tidy Up

* * *

"One of the things we learned in my family was how to wash clothes and how to clean house. It was a requirement in my house growing up and it is a requirement in my own house. If I walk in your house and can write on your table, you're sloppy."
—Bill Holloman

How to Clean Your House

Step 1: Straighten up. Make your bed, for starters. It sets the tone for not only your home, but also your day ahead. Then fold and return any crumpled clothes to their hangers, shelves, or drawers, and toss the dirties in your hamper. (In case you're wondering, if you've worn a pair of underpants once, consider them dirty, even if they don't *look* dirty. Do not turn them inside out and wear them again. That's a cardinal rule, and if you choose to break it, you will officially be gross.) Drop any loose change in a designated jar, labeled LIFT TICKETS, WEEKEND IN PARIS, or HOT-DATE FUND, and file away any mail and magazines.

Step 2: Dust. You're going to need to polish, or at least wipe clean, every surface (at least the noticeable ones). First, remove any stuff you have sitting on top of your dining room table, sideboards, nightstands, vanities, or bar. Then spray the surface with the appropriate cleaner and wipe away the dust, using a clean rag, a soft old T-shirt, or a paper towel.

Step 3: Vacuum. If you're reading this expecting instructions on how to vacuum, then you're just procrastinating. Go on now. Get on with it!

Step 4: Disinfect. Somebody's got to clean the bathroom, and it's that person you see staring back at you in your toothpaste-splotched mirror. Scrub-a-dub-dub the tub and the walls of the shower with a mild abrasive and brush or sponge. Wipe down the sink, mirror, and toilet seat. Finally, lift the toilet seat, squirt some cleaner in the bowl (or better yet, pour in a cup of white vinegar), scrub the bowl and the underside of the toilet seat with a long-handled brush, and let it sit before flushing.

Step 5: Invite company over, and when they start doling out the compliments, put your thumbs in your pockets, rock on your heels, and pretend your place always looks so nice. Aw, yeah.

More Handy Tips

- Dust from top to bottom, or you'll constantly be working against yourself.

- If you've got a good vacuum, you may be able to get away with using one of the fancy attachments to dust almost everything. Go ahead and give it a try—just not on a table full of your sweetie's Precious Moments figurines.

- You could buy fancy cleaning supplies, but they cost big bucks and many are lousy for the environment. Instead, use white vinegar to clean and disinfect most surfaces, including countertops, windows, even toilets.

Tame Your Turf

. . .

"Grass always grows, so you have to take care of it. Otherwise, it gets away from you. In Cleveland, if you didn't mow your lawn, they used to send a policeman along to remind you that it's out of whack."
—JOE BABIN

HOW TO MOW A LAWN

Step 1: Walk your land. Pick up any sticks, rocks, forgotten golf clubs, lonely baseball gloves, or any other items that might hurt or get hurt by your mower.

Step 2: Check your mower. Make sure your blades are sharp and anything squeaky gets oil. Fill the tank, if you're using a gas mower.

Step 3: Adjust your blade height. No matter how long your grass is, never mow off more than a third of its height at once, or you risk damaging your lawn. Most grasses will do well at about two to three inches tall, though Bermuda and bent grasses like to be a touch shorter.

Step 4: Snip away. Starting at one edge of your lawn, push or ride your mower in a straight line to the opposite edge. Then turn your mower around and return from whence you came, mowing the strip of lawn adjacent to your first pass. Allow your strips to overlap by a few inches to avoid any hairy patches, and of course watch out for trees! You've got to go around them. Repeat until your lawn is neatly shorn.

Step 5: Clean up the edges. If necessary, take an edger or trimmer and zip along the edges of your sidewalk and driveway.

Step 6: Knock on the back door and ask someone inside to bring you a nice cold one. You've earned it.

More Handy Tips

- For best results, mow your lawn once a week when it's dry, either in the late morning or early evening.

- Vary your mowing pattern each week so your grass grows vertically and you don't get tire tracks in your lawn.

- Be considerate of your neighbors. Nobody wants to be woken up to the sound of you mowing your lawn, especially on a lazy Sunday morning.

- Sharpen the blades on your mower once a year for a cleaner cut and healthier grass.

- If you cut your grass too short, it'll only grow back faster, sacrificing its own root health to do so. The only time you may go shorter than usual is during your last mow before snowfall.

- Longer grass helps the water stay in the soil longer, giving you a greener lawn.

- Skip the raking. Your grass clippings will act as a natural fertilizer.

- Watch out for tree roots. Nicking them with your mower blades could damage your tree.

- Be careful. Wear sunscreen, goggles, and hearing protection, if necessary. Keep small children and pets away from you while you work. And use caution while mowing hills.

Roll Out

• • •

"I got caught one night with a blowout. I had a pair of canvas gloves, and I stuffed them in the hole in the tire, put the spare tube back in that thing, pumped it up by hand, and went back home."
—Philip Spooner

How to Change a Flat Tire

Step 1: Stay calm. If you get a flat, you'll know it by the telltale *thlump-thlump-thlump* sound of driving on deflated rubber. There's no need to swerve, slam on the brakes, or scream. Take a deep breath, slow down, and turn on your blinking hazard lights.

Step 2: Pull over as soon as possible. Drive to a safe, flat, hard place as far away as you can from traffic, throw your car in park (or leave it in first, if you're old-school and driving a stick shift), activate your emergency brake, and ask your passengers, if you have any, to get out of the car and stand in a safe place. Light flares, if you've got 'em and know how to light them safely, and place them a good seventy-five feet behind your car. Then figure out which tire bit the dust and curse it, especially if you're wearing nice clothes, you're in a rush, or it's raining. Finally, if you can find one, place a large rock or piece of wood behind the diagonally opposite tire.

Step 3: Pop the trunk. Usually, that's where you'll find everything you need to get back on the road—a spare tire (or a dinko doughnut tire, which will at least get you to the nearest service station), a jack, and a lug wrench. If you don't see these tools at first glance, you might have to lift up the carpet in your trunk. (If you're driving a pickup truck, look behind the seat for your gear.)

Step 4: Find your lug nuts. If you can see them in the center of your wheel, skip to step 5. If not, you'll have to first pop your hubcap. To do so, slip the flat end of your lug wrench beneath the edge of your hubcap and pry it off.

Step 5: Go nuts. Place the other end of your lug wrench on each of the nuts, and loosen—but don't remove!—the nuts by turning your wrench in a counterclockwise motion. Remember, lefty-loosey, righty-tighty. Those nuts are going to be as tight as can be, so really muscle your wrench. Try grunting, if you think it'll help or make you look tough.

Step 6: Jack it up. Refer to your owner's manual for the proper positioning, and then turn the crank until your car is high enough off the ground to remove the tire. Yeah, that's right. You just single-handedly lifted your car.

Step 7: Change your tire. Screw off the loose nuts and put them in a safe place, then slide off your flat tire and set it aside. Slide on your spare tire flush against the hub, lining up the studs with the holes, replace the lug nuts, and tighten them by hand, mustering all the finger strength you amassed from those many years of thumb wrestling.

Step 8: Lower your car. Wind down your jack until all four wheels are on the ground. Using your wrench, tighten each lug nut as much as you possibly can, but don't go in a circle. Tighten one, then do the opposite one, and so forth. How tightly? Let's just say veins should be popping out of your forehead.

Step 9: Dab the sweat off your brow.

Step 10: Toss everything in the trunk, including your hubcap, jack, wrench, and flatty. Load up your passengers, if you've got any, and extinguish any flares.

Step 11: Drive slowly (and proudly) to your nearest service station, where you can get a full-sized replacement tire.

More Handy Tips

- Never attempt to change a tire on a hill or soft ground, or your car could fall or roll on you, and then you'd be flat, too.

- Check the wall of your spare tire for any speed limitations.

- If you get a flat in a dangerous area or one that just gives you the heebie-jeebies, drive slowly to the nearest service station or public place. You may ruin your wheel, but at least you'll be safe.

- A well-lit public parking lot is the best place to change a flat. Get to one, if you can.

- Cars are really heavy, duh. If you're not sure you can jack it up and put a new wheel on properly, ask for help when doing it. You'll become a master in no time, um, flat.

Get Greasy

. . .

*"You can change the oil. It's not difficult, and you can save money and have
an interesting chore and the satisfaction of knowing you've done it.
Do you know why ditchdiggers get more satisfaction than anyone else
at the end the day? Because the ditchdigger can turn around
and see all the dirt he threw out."*

—Chuck Tatum

How to Change the Oil

Step 1: Slip into a jumpsuit, preferably one that has a patch with
your name on it sewn above the pocket. No jumpsuit? Old cruddy
clothes and a trucker hat will be fine, then. You're going to get a little
dirty. Then blast the radio, preferably a country or metal station, for
full effect.

Step 2: Read your owner's manual. Okay, so this step is a little anti-
climactic, but it's important. Your owner's manual will tell you what
kind of oil and filter your car needs, whether you need a new drain plug
gasket, and how much oil you need to buy.

Step 3: Gather your supplies. You'll need oil and a new filter, a funnel, a drain pan, a socket wrench, an oil filter wrench that matches the
size of your filter, a rag, a good pair of gloves, and, depending on your
car, a new drain plug gasket.

Step 4: Get your car in the right spot. Take it for a few spins around the block first, because warmer oil drains faster than cold oil. Once your engine is toasty, park your car on a level surface, turn it off, and set the emergency brake. Better throw some cardboard, newspaper, or a tarp underneath in case you make a mess.

Step 5: Pop the hood, unscrew the oil fill cap, and set it in a safe place. It'll help the oil drain faster.

Step 6: Locate your drain plug. Slide under the car with a flashlight and look for the lowest item on the engine. You'll see a decently sized nut with a washer around it that, if you're lucky, says DRAIN PLUG on it. You'll know you have the right one if the metal around it is warm. If the metal is cold, you're probably looking at the slightly larger drain plug for the transmission fluid. Whatever you do, don't pull that one!

Step 7: Drain the oil. The oil will shoot out of its reservoir with great gusto, so put your pan (or a bucket) underneath the plug and, using a socket wrench, turn the plug counterclockwise until it comes loose. Here comes the oil! It'll take at least two minutes for it to completely drain. Once it stops flowing, replace the plug (and gasket if necessary), tightening it first by hand, and then with your socket wrench.

Step 8: Replace the filter. It looks like a palm-sized cylinder, and it'll be located either just above the oil pan underneath your car or under the hood somewhere. You may have to hunt for it, and even possibly remove a decorative shield to get to it. Using your filter wrench, loosen the filter and then unscrew it with your hand. Take your new filter out of the box, lube up the top of it with some new oil, and screw it into place with your hand.

Step 9: Boredom check. How's the radio station working out for you? Not good? Change it to NPR, listen to *Car Talk*, and feel superior to all those schmucks calling in, okay?

Step 10: Fill 'er up. Pop the hood of your engine, drop the funnel in the oil fill hole, add your new oil, and screw on the cap again. Hopefully, you didn't lose it.

Step 11: Warm 'er up. Turn your engine on and let it idle. Careful you don't get your seats dirty! After a few minutes, turn it back off, then check under the car for any leakage.

Step 12: Check the oil level. Pull the dipstick out, wipe it off on something other than your own pants, dip it back into the reservoir once more, and then pull it out for a look-see. It should be at the FULL mark. If it's shy, add more oil.

Step 13: Clean up. Gather your tools and pour the dirty oil into an old plastic milk jug. It's illegal to pour it down the drain or into the ground, because it will contaminate your water. Take it to a recycling center. Many quick-lube joints will take it off your hands for no charge.

More Handy Tips

- Change your oil and oil filter about every five thousand miles. Pushing it any longer will only up your chances of breaking your car in, no doubt, some very expensive way. It needs good oil to run properly.

- Check your oil levels every few hundred miles.

- If you can't fit under your car, use two jack stands (not just a jack!) to raise it up. Or, if you have help, drive the front two wheels of your car onto ramps and place chocks behind the back two wheels. Always engage your emergency brake!

- If you're scratching your head after step 1, find a grease monkey to mentor you. He'll show you how to do it safely, and you can buy him a cold one afterward.

Talk Shop

• • •

"The only way to find a good mechanic is to talk to the guys in the neighborhood. You've got to ask your friends, because some mechanics will rip you off."
—AL SULKA

HOW TO COMMUNICATE WITH A MECHANIC

Step 1: Smile. This may be difficult to do if your car is broken and you know it's going to cost you some bucks to get it fixed. Still, it's not likely your mechanic's fault, and if you walk into the garage with a chip on your shoulder, you probably won't inspire the best possible service.

Step 2: Describe the problem in detail. Even if your mechanic doesn't ask (as he should), be sure to offer up all the pertinent information. Tell him when the problem started, when it happens (at high or low speed, in hot or cold weather, when your blinker is on), and what it sounds or feels like. Don't be afraid to unleash your onomatopoeia, as in, "When I slow down, my car goes *blerp blop poop voop voop voop bang fizzle.*" You may feel silly, but he may also know exactly what you're talking about, and the less time he has to spend diagnosing the problem, the lower your bill will be.

Step 3: Ask for an estimate. Once your mechanic pinpoints the problem, request that he call you with a ballpark figure for the parts and labor before proceeding. If it's too expensive, you can make the decision to put off the repair or do only enough to get your car running.

If it's within your budget, at least you'll be mentally prepared to see the bill when you pick it up.

Step 4: Request to see the discarded parts. It'll only make you feel better about spending your hard-earned money if, for example, you can see with your own two eyes just how rusty your rotors actually were. Most reputable mechanics will be happy to show you.

More Handy Tips

- Ask your friends if they have a mechanic they know and trust. When it comes to car repair, there's nothing better than a word-of-mouth recommendation.

- When you're dropping your car off for repairs, tidy up the interior. Nobody wants to spend time working on a car that smells like a two-week-old Big Mac wrapper.

- If you're happy with your mechanic's work, tell him so, and remind him you'll be sending your friends his way. It helps foster a good relationship that'll last for years to come.

Hit the Road

. . .

*"When I was twelve, my mother sold our property, bought a 1936
Terraplane, and drove it from Oklahoma to California. There were seven of
us in this one car. She packed the floor of the backseat higher and higher and
then put a mattress over it so the young kids could sleep. Oh, they loved it!
She was a genius at packing that car."*
—Chuck Tatum

HOW TO PACK A CAR

Step 1: Clean out your vehicle. You're not going to be able to fit too
much junk in your trunk if you're already hauling around your old hiking boots, a soccer ball, a bunch of empty water bottles, and that box of
books once destined for the used-book store. Before you can load up,
you've got to load out.

Step 2: Take inventory of the big stuff. If you're packing any long
items, like a snowboard or skis, inside the car, take into account that
you'll have to put the backseat down to slide them through the trunk.
If you're packing unwieldy items, like a table or chairs, disassemble
what you can before loading, so they're more maneuverable.

Step 3: Divvy up the small stuff. Remember, because you're driving,
not flying, you won't be charged a fee for every bag you pack, so there's
no need to cram all your belongings into one giant suitcase. Think
about it: You may not be able to fit two large suitcases in your trunk,
but you will probably be able to fit one big one, along with two duffel

bags, filled with the same stuff. The smaller the items, the more flexibility you'll have with your space.

Step 4: Carry everything to the car. Try to enjoy the heavy lifting while you're at it. You're about to sit still for a very long time, so relish this moment when you can stretch your legs and feel your blood pumping.

Step 5: Load up. Pop the trunk and drop in the biggest stuff first. If you're having trouble fitting something, work the angles. Sometimes a small rotation or a slight twist as you slide it in can help, and since the car is still empty, you have plenty of room to operate. (Having another person help guide it from the other side can help, too, but only if that person is willing to listen to you and try your ideas, at least at first. Two lead packers per car is one too many.) Once you've got the large items in, squeeze the smaller stuff into any remaining open spaces.

Step 6: Place anything you may need en route inside the car: your wallet, sunglasses, music, snacks, books, toys, an empty trash bag, and a first-aid kit.

Step 7: Check your work. Sit in the driver's seat and make sure you've got a clear view out of all your windows and in all your mirrors. Also make sure all necessary seat belts are accessible.

Step 8: Buckle up and hit the road. Happy driving!

More Handy Tips

- If you've got the time and a secure place to park, pack the night before. It always takes a little (or a lot) longer than you anticipate, and if you get it done, you'll be more likely to depart on schedule.

- Don't put anything on the back windowsill of your car. If you get in an accident, even something small could turn into a deadly projectile. How tragic would it be if you were actually killed by a bobblehead?

- If you're using a rooftop carrier, never fill it more than eighteen inches high and never let it exceed a hundred pounds or you'll increase your risk of rolling over on sharp turns.

- Wondering how much your car can safely haul? Open your door and read the sticker inside. It'll tell you the maximum load.

- Fill your tires with air before you hit the road. Not only will it make for a safer ride, but you'll also improve your gas mileage by more than 3 percent. Woo hoo!

3

Leading

. . .

Set a good example, even when no one is watching.
Living honorably is as much for you as it is
for those who look up to you.

Soldier On

. . .

"Most of my missions in World War II were escorting bomber planes. We were just average Americans trying to protect our country. Being afraid will clutter up your mind. Your mind has to be clear."
—BILL HOLLOMAN

HOW TO BE BRAVE

Step 1: Assess the situation. Before you tackle anything (or anyone), step back for a moment and rationally take in all necessary information. Whether you are giving your first public speech, walking alone at night in a dangerous forest (or city), fighting in a schoolyard (or international) conflict, you've got to be smart. Understand your surroundings, know your strengths and weaknesses, and have a clear objective.

Step 2: Prepare yourself for greatness. There's a reason "practice makes perfect" is an oft-repeated idiom. It's actually true. Even seemingly insurmountable situations become doable if you've trained for them. The more you practice anything, the braver you'll feel in the real situation.

Step 3: Take action. Do, don't think. Focus on the steps to achieving your goal and let your body carry you through. If you've prepared, it'll know exactly what to do. Still having trouble quieting your mind? Replace those potentially paralyzing "what-ifs" with a new, more definitive mantra, like, "I can do this."

Step 4: Embrace your fear. Because it'll trigger a release of adrenaline in your body, it'll increase your heart rate, send blood to your muscles, and give you energy you never even knew you had. (Translation: It works way better than a Red Bull at slapping you awake.) So use your fear, and your body's reaction to it, to your advantage, and know that it's giving you everything you physically need to fight well or flee fast. Don't be ashamed of being a little (or even a lot) scared, either. Bravery and fearlessness aren't synonyms. Bravery means you fear and do it anyway. Besides, only fools (or liars) are never afraid.

Step 5: Reach down. Connect your mission to your deeper beliefs—in humanity, love, freedom, nature, God, your family, whatever works for you. Remembering who you are and why you're doing what you're doing will embolden you. If you know in your heart that you are just and your cause is noble, you can pull from that belief, and it will make you brave.

More Handy Tips

- There is a fine line between bravery and stupidity. Sometimes the bravest thing to do is to step back from a situation and better prepare yourself so you tackle it wisely.

- A brave person seeks to elevate and honor, rather than diminish or degrade, those around him. If you try to prove your strength or fearlessness by hurting or bullying someone weaker than you, then you're a coward, not a hero.

- Defend others. Sometimes standing up for someone else, merely thinking about his needs instead of your own, makes you a stronger person.

Bring Home the Bacon

. . .

"The money isn't all yours to spend on yourself. I always felt that I needed to work hard enough to see that my family was taken care of and that's what I tried to do—to save."
—CHUCK TATUM

HOW TO SUPPORT YOUR FAMILY

Step 1: Set goals. By adding meaning to your work, you'll be more likely to stay committed to it and even enjoy it. Divide a piece of paper in half, and mark one column IN ONE YEAR and the other IN FIVE YEARS. Then jot down some financial and life goals you'd like to achieve in those time spans. Consider your career, your savings, your home, your kids' education, any vacations you'd like to take. Whenever you're lagging in the energy or enthusiasm departments, refer to your list to feel reinvigorated. However hokey it sounds, it'll be a huge thrill to systematically reach each goal you set for yourself.

Step 2: Stay focused. Even if you don't currently have your dream job—you might be delivering pizzas when you want to be a chef or pushing pencils when you want to be in charge—find something to be passionate about in your work. Then, take a deep breath and know that you'll reach your goals, if you just keep your nose down and work hard. If you're the best at what you're doing now, you'll advance in no time.

Step 3: Rally the team. Share your financial plans and hopes with your partner and children. That way, they won't think of money as something that magically appears, and they'll learn the value of a hard day's work. Also, you'll feel like a team, working together to meet your goals, especially if you set a few the whole crew can look forward to, like a trip to Dollywood. (Hey, don't knock it until you try it. Dolly Parton rules.)

Step 4: Frame it. Keep a photo of your family at your office. If you're having a hard day, look at that picture and reset your mind. People are depending on you.

More Handy Tips

- Just because you are filling the family coffers doesn't mean that you're off the hook around the house. Don't let all the domestic stuff fall on your partner, who's probably working, too. You share the work outside the home. Share it inside as well.

- If you have kids, don't become a walking checkbook. Buying them the fanciest baseball glove may win their squeals, but showing up at the game will win their hearts.

Switch Hats

• • •

"Don't chase the almighty dollar. It's not that important. And make your home a home, a place where everyone wants to be, a place where everyone gets along."
—BILL HOLLOMAN

HOW TO LEAVE WORK AT WORK

Step 1: Create a buffer zone. Whether you take scenic, windy back roads rather than the highway, or a walk around the block after you get off the train, give yourself a few minutes to decompress before you call out, "Honey, I'm home!" The daily ritual will help send a signal to your brain that it's time to shift gears.

Step 2: Listen. Instead of walking in and venting about your day to anyone within earshot, try asking your family how their day was first. If their troubles seem insignificant compared with yours, well, good. You want their troubles to be tiny. Celebrate their triumphs and console them for their disappointments, and you'll find whatever was stressing you will fall away. If it doesn't, talk about it with your partner, but set a time limit for your bellyaching. Fifteen minutes of venting helps clear the air. Five hours of venting just pollutes it.

Step 3: Disconnect. Sure, there'll be occasions when you have to work at night or on weekends. That's understandable. What's not? Keeping your BlackBerry on your armrest while you're watching *Modern Family* or walking around with a Bluetooth in your ear at your kid's soccer game. If you never disconnect from the office, your work will follow you everywhere and your family or friends will never feel like a priority. When you're out, be out.

Step 4: Be grateful. Not to get too terribly morbid, but nobody ever says on his deathbed, "I just wish I spent more time in the office." Life is too short to spend in a cubicle or tethered to your work via cell phone and email. Remember to be thankful for all the other things that are important to you: your family, your friends, hiking, beer brewing, whatever brings you joy. You may have to give your job forty hours a week, but you don't owe anyone your life.

More Handy Tips

- If you just can't get work out of your head, get it out of your body. Go for a run, lift weights, chop wood. Once those endorphins kick in, you'll feel better in no time.

- If you're lucky enough to have someone lovely meet you at the door with your slippers and a fresh cocktail, then life is good. Just don't overdo it with the martinis, or you'll simply be trading one mind-numbing place (your office) for another (drunk town). You've got to be in the right head to enjoy the good stuff at home, too.

- Remember that your life is not solely defined by your work. Sacrificing all your time and energy on work alone won't make you successful; it'll make you boring and unhappy. Strive to live a well-rounded life. Don't work all your days away.

Dry Tears

• • •

"Sometimes a hug means more than anything you can say."
—AL SULKA

HOW TO COMFORT A LOVED ONE

Step 1: Be there. When you know your loved one is upset, don't avoid or confront her. Just be available and ready to listen when she's ready to talk.

Step 2: Offer a shoulder. Even if you don't think there's anything you can do to make your loved one feel better, asking if you can help can make all the difference. Float the idea and see if she'll accept. Then be prepared to hear what she has to say, and rather than immediately offering advice or trying to fix what ails her, validate her feelings and show her that you understand.

Step 3: Be patient. Continuing to comfort your loved one beyond the time *you* think she should have bounced back can be a challenge. Just remember that everyone heals at their own pace, and ultimately you want your loved one to thoroughly work through her emotions so she can be happy.

Step 4: Offer encouragement. Remind her of how much you love and appreciate her, and set a good example of looking on the bright side. Your joy and strength can elevate those around you.

More Handy Tips

- You don't have to fully understand what your friend or family member is going through to be supportive. Just because you don't feel her pain doesn't mean she shouldn't, either.

- You've got to take care of yourself first in order to be able to take care of others. If you need support, too, reach out to your own friends, family members, or even a professional. You don't have to go it alone.

- If all else fails, try to make her laugh. Turn to page 253 to learn how to tell a clean joke.

Do the Right Thing

• • •

"I still haven't come to a conclusion as to what life is about other than this: Strive to do the right thing. Use the golden rule as your cornerstone. It's most beneficial to humanity."
—Buck Buchanan

HOW TO BE A ROLE MODEL

Step 1: Always be yourself. When you have confidence in the skills or qualities that make you an individual, you'll earn respect and admiration from others. Authenticity, and having the integrity to be who you are, is something to be admired.

Step 2: Find consistency. Those who look up to you will learn as much from you when you're "teaching" them as when you aren't. Be aware of yourself at all times, show off your strengths, and be mindful of your weaknesses.

Step 3: Be generous. It's not your success that determines what sort of leader you can be. It's how you handle that success. Be humble in your achievements and quick to share credit where it is due.

More Handy Tips

- Never bully or look down on others who don't enjoy your good fortune.
- Imagine who you'd like your role model to be, or who you would've wanted as a child, and be that person. You can be your own role model.

Be Critical

* * *

"Turn off your TV and think for yourself."
—Al Sulka

How to Think about Politics

Step 1: Get educated. Our government is run by the people (that's you!) for the people (hello, you again!). So to participate in a meaningful way, first you've got to know what's going on. Go to your local town hall meetings, read your newspaper, talk to your neighbors, write to your congressional representatives, heck, even watch C-SPAN. *Politics* may seem like a word that describes old white guys in suits arguing over things that don't affect you, but that's not true at all. Well, at least the part about it not affecting you. Every vote matters in a very real way. You should know where you stand.

Step 2: Find balance. Just because a news channel calls itself "fair and balanced" or "most trusted" doesn't mean it's actually true. But how would you know any different if that's the only viewpoint you ever hear? Get your information from as many different newspapers, TV shows, radio programs, and websites as possible. If you're watching Glenn Beck every night, turn to Rachel Maddow every once in a while for a new perspective. Getting your news from the "right" and "left" doesn't make you disloyal to your party, but it does prove that you're an independent thinker, not a puppet. Consider all sides to every story before making up your mind on how you feel about it.

Step 3: Check facts. Never parrot things you hear or read without first checking the source, and then checking the facts. (A great resource: www.factcheck.org.) Before you repeat what you heard on talk radio or at the local pub, first ask yourself: What does this person have invested in making this statement? Does it financially benefit him in some way? Does she have a personal bias? Is it really about something else? Nothing will make you look more foolish than repeating false statements or passing on vitriol when you don't know the facts.

Step 4: Honor difference. While everyone claims they know the founders' intent, one thing is indisputable: This country wasn't founded on just one idea from one person. We came together from all different places and backgrounds to form a union, and our differences are what make us strong. Appreciate one another, listen, put forth ideas (not accusations), and we'll all be better off for it.

More Handy Tips

- Just because you *can* talk about politics doesn't mean you should do it all the time. While there is often room for healthy debate between friends, there's a time and place for everything.

- Name-calling and ridiculing say much more about you than they do anyone else. Always be respectful of your fellow citizens, and never ever resort to violence.

- To find out exactly what the federal government is up to, visit www.gpoaccess.gov. There you can find the Congressional Record, the full text of all laws, bills, and budgets.

Keep Safe

• • •

"First, you have to be able to take care of yourself. Then you can take care of your family. Intelligence will get you further than anything else."
—ANGEL RODRIGUEZ

HOW TO PROTECT YOUR HOME

Step 1: Befriend your neighbors. Having a couple of extra sets of friendly eyes on your home may help secure it better than any high-tech burglar alarm. Get to know the people in your neighborhood and look out for one another. Collect one another's mail when you're on vacation, and be mindful of any funny business, like a dodgy fella parked outside. It takes more than one person to make a safe neighborhood.

Step 2: Vary your schedule. The more predictable your days and nights, the easier a target you are. Even if your home is empty from nine to five every day and for the entire month of August when you stay at your in-laws' lake cottage, make it look like someone is home all the time. Keep your garage door closed and set your lights on a timer.

Step 3: Secure doors and windows. Make sure they're properly installed and always locked. And install a light outside (motion detector lights work best) so you can see what's going on if necessary.

Step 4: Live modestly. If you've worked hard and have the savings, there's nothing wrong with buying and having nice things. Just don't brag about it by positioning all your bling—your Bose speakers, your new iPad, your flat-screen TV—so it's viewable from the street. That may only invite ne'er-do-wells.

More Handy Tips

- Keep your whereabouts private. Don't post a note on your front door announcing to your postman (and potential burglars) that you'll be gone through next week. If your neighbor can't collect your mail, call your post office and ask them to hold it for you.

- Don't post your vacation plans online. Sure, your Facebook or Twitter friends will be impressed with your travels, but they can hear all about it, and see your photos, too, when you get home.

- If you have a gun, keep it in a safe. Locking it up will only help protect you and your family.

- Invest in homeowner's or renter's insurance, so you'll know your home and valuables will be covered if anything goes wrong. Find the best plan for you, and always keep it up to date.

- If all else fails, get a dog. A well-trained watchdog beats any alarm system. A lapdog might work, too, but only if your intruder can be killed by cuteness.

Cope Well

. . .

"Accept the fact that the bad news is coming at you and try and figure out how best to minimize the risk. When you don't really know what to do, ask for help. If you don't do that, you're not being fair to yourself or anybody else."
—FRANK WALTER

HOW TO HANDLE BAD NEWS

Step 1: Meet it head-on. Whether on not you had prior warning that bad news was coming, don't hide from it. Take it with your chin up. Anyone can handle good news well, but the strength of your character is judged by how you handle the not-so-good news.

Step 2: Talk about it. Many people try to hide their misfortune from others out of shame or embarrassment or an urge to "protect," but isolation only makes it sting more. Seek comfort from your friends or family. They'll reassure you of their love and support, and you'll feel emboldened to move on.

Step 3: Take charge. If your bad news came from your boss, your sweetie, your doctor, or your financial adviser, the situation was likely beyond your control. Let's have a quick moment of silence for how much that bites the big one. Okay, take a deep breath and know this: You've got more control of the situation now. Hey, at least you know about it. That's a good start. Next, educate yourself. Learn all that you can about what happened, how to get beyond it, and how to ensure that it doesn't happen again. You must take responsibility for what happens next.

Step 4: Look at the bright side. Whatever the bad news, you're still here and you're reading this book, which is at least sort of fun, right? And chances are, someone else has had it much worse. So try not to wallow in your pain. Instead, look around you, take stock of the good things, and give thanks for what you *do* have.

More Handy Tips

- A nip of whiskey may take the initial sting away, but too many nips will only leave you with a pounding headache, plus whatever upset you in the first place. If you're going to drink to soften the blow, do it in moderation.

- If you think you need more serious help, there's no shame in that. To find a certified psychologist near you, visit http://locator.apa .org.

Pull Yourself Up

* * *

"When I was a teenager, we had to saw our own wood for the stove. After you'd do enough, you'd start to get tired, but you had to finish up the cord of wood. So you'd bow your neck and saw wood. You knew you had to go on. Most of my ventures have been not quite a success. How do I bounce back? Grit my teeth, bow my neck, and saw wood."
— Buck Buchanan

HOW TO BOUNCE BACK AFTER FAILURE

Step 1: Be proud that you took a chance. So things didn't go your way, at least not this time, but you tried and that surely counts for something. The path to success is rarely a straight line. Just think, the great ballplayer Babe Ruth didn't hit all those homers without a miss. In fact, the Bronx bomber struck out a whopping 1,330 times while at bat. The writer J. K. Rowling was divorced, unemployed, and as broke as can be when she wrote the first of the Harry Potter books. And after sending out her manuscript, it was rejected by multiple publishers before one lucky (or insightful) editor finally picked it up. And you? What will your story be? Here's a start: You've failed, and you're still here, still standing, still searching for something better. That officially makes you awesome.

Step 2: Figure out what you did wrong. Think of your failure as a learning experience. It's a building block necessary for your ultimate success. At least now you know what not to do, and the next time around you'll be that much smarter and therefore that much likelier to succeed. Lesson learned. Advantage, you.

Step 3: Figure out what you did right. Make a list of all the good decisions you made, positive attributes you brought, ideas you had that helped advance your project. Just because it didn't pan out this time doesn't mean it won't ever, and just because your project failed doesn't mean you are a failure. Separate the two ideas.

Step 4: Try again. You can do it!

More Handy Tips

- Visualize success. As difficult as it may be, close your eyes and imagine yourself doing exactly what you set out to do. It'll make it that much closer.

- Ask for help, if you need it. If you're having a hard time pulling yourself out of your misery, your friends may be able to help. Plan a get-together, and do something fun. Or at least get some hugs.

- Celebrate what you do have, whether it's your health, your family, your home, your dog, or even that you've got one more great day to rock this joint.

Give Everything

· · ·

"We are creatures of habit. Your body adapts to hard work.
Don't be afraid of it."
—ANGEL RODRIGUEZ

HOW TO WORK HARD

Step 1: Motivate. When your alarm goes off in the morning, it's up to you, buddy. No one else can pull you out of bed but you. Even before your morning joe (see page 232), start each day with a dose of self-discipline. Draw from within, get up, get out, and take on the world.

Step 2: Set goals. Start small and go big: From hourly to daily to monthly to yearly, remind yourself of your goals throughout the day. Make a list if you can, and cross each off as you surpass it. There is little in life that is more satisfying than crossing off one goal (and writing another).

Step 3: Love the burn. When things get harder, don't give up. Instead, when you feel like you've almost reached the breaking point, recognize the feeling (whether it's "OW!" or "I'm tired" or "My brain hurts") and work through it. Tell yourself that's when everyone else quits. And by even reaching that point, you've already bested the majority.

Step 4: Play hard. After you put in a hard day's work, reward yourself in some way. It'll give you something to look forward to, and help make it all seem worth it.

More Handy Tips

- Remember, whatever your field or goal, talent means almost nothing. There are millions of naturally talented athletes sitting on their couches, eating chips, while watching the big game, and only a few stars on the field. Talent may open the door, but experience, practice, and hard work are the only ways to achieve greatness.

4

Prospering

. . .

*Work hard, look smart, save well and
you'll always be secure.*

Power Up

* * *

"If you don't have a suit, you look like a bum."
—AL SULKA

HOW TO BUY A SUIT

Step 1: Go for a classic. Unless you already have a closet full of suits, you'll need at least one good one that's as versatile as possible. Keep in mind that fashions change, so don't get suckered into the latest trend or talked into a crazy three-piece purple number. As you add to your wardrobe, you can experiment with other styles, but for now just go to a department store that fits your budget and start browsing.

Step 2: Know the anatomy of a suit. When you're flipping through the racks, keep your eye out for these four major style markers:

The fabric: Buy a lightweight wool suit, which, unlike cotton or linen, can be worn year-round. Go for a darker color, if you're hefty; a lighter color, if you're skinny; and vertical stripes, if you're short. Above all, avoid poly-blends, unless you plan on selling used cars. Polyester suits turn shiny.

The buttons: You can't go wrong with the always-stylish two-button suit. A one-buttoner is retro eighties, which you can rock with the right haircut. A three-buttoner is retro nineties, which you can rock if you're tall and thin. If you're at all unsure, go for the two-fer.

The vents: Your suit should have at least one. Without a vent, your bottom will be busting out of your jacket in a way that will hurt the eyes of the people behind you. Choose a jacket with a center vent, if you're tall or hefty; or double side vents, if you're vertically challenged or plan on faking a British accent anytime soon. Side vents are big in Europe.

The lapel: For a classic look, choose one with a V-shaped notch. Your other option is a wider peak lapel, which, if done correctly, can add some flair, or if done poorly, can make you look like a seventies porn star.

Step 3: Get a perfect fit. Try on several suits, and besides trying to raise your arms above your head and sit down without blowing a button, look for these other guidelines to a good fit:

The shoulders: They should end at the end of your shoulder. If they extend beyond your shoulder, the suit is too big and the fabric will wrinkle. If they fall short, the jacket is too small.

The chest: With the suit buttoned, you should be able to just barely slip your closed fist between your chest and jacket. If you can fit more than your fist, it's too big. If you can't fit your fist at all, it's probably too snug, Mr. Muscles.

The length: Stand with your arms at your sides. The jacket should end at your knuckles, and you should be able to wrap your fingers underneath it. If you have to bend your arms to do so, it's too short. If it ends at your knees, it's too long.

The sleeves: The cuffs should fall where your wrists meet your hands, and a quarter inch of your shirt cuff should be showing through the bottom.

The pants: Wear them at your hips, no higher, no lower. If they catch wind when you walk, they're too big. And when you wear them with shoes, the material should fall on top of your laces, and break, or create a horizontal crease, about one inch from the bottom. Nobody should see your socks.

Step 4: Hire a tailor. Even if you think the suit fits pretty perfectly at the store, ask a tailor to fine-tune it for you. By the time he's done, it'll fit your every curve like a custom-made suit, and you'll look like a million bucks. After he makes the alterations, try on the suit once more before you leave the store to ensure its perfection. Then wear it with pride, confident that you look as sharp as can be.

More Handy Tips

- Bring a second pair of eyes. Some suit salesmen work on commission, so while they often have good advice, it helps to have a stylish, straight-shooting friend with you who can give you an honest opinion before you buy anything.

- Wear a dress shirt and shoes when suit shopping. You won't be able to tell how a suit truly fits if you're wearing a sweatshirt and sneaks with it.

- Take care of your investment. Decent suits aren't cheap, so treat them well. If you're just starting out, buy two good ones and alternate them, being sure to hang them up between wears.

- Never throw a suit in the washing machine. These babies need to be dry-cleaned.

- Dress down a good jacket with jeans, a T-shirt, and super-fly sneakers on weekends.

Earn More

• • •

"Set your goal and have that feeling of accomplishment. Earn your stature. Get a career and progress. If you're successful, there's nothing better."
—Bob Kelly

How to Get a Raise

Step 1: Work hard. Before you even think of asking for more money, prove to yourself and your boss that you're worth more than your current salary. Take on more work, shoulder more responsibility, show initiative, and keep a positive attitude. You need to make yourself invaluable before you ask for extra love.

Step 2: Master your timing. Don't waltz into your boss's office immediately after your company has suffered a major loss or been sold to new owners. Instead, do it when times are good or after you've hit a home run.

Step 3: Make your case. The fact that the landlord just jacked up your rent, or your daughter needs braces, or you really want to go to Tulúm with your sweetie this summer means absolutely nothing to your boss, and bringing those things up will only make you seem icky and unprofessional. Instead, begin the conversation by listing your actual accomplishments and quantifiable successes. For instance, "I brought us 20 percent more business last quarter."

Step 4: Shoot for the stars. Ask for more than you expect. If you'd be happy with a 10 percent raise, ask for 15 or 20 percent. Negotiating means both parties must be flexible, and if you both feel you've given a little, you'll both feel successful.

Step 5: Have a backup plan. When times are tough, companies may not be able to offer a raise to anyone. If it's clear that they really can't afford to pay you more, ask for other perks, like more vacation time, a flexible workweek, or a performance-based bonus, that will make your life better. These things might make you happy without hurting their books, so everyone wins.

More Handy Tips

- You deserve to be paid what you're worth. If this particular company can't (or won't) pay you fairly, keep your chin up, keep working hard, and look for another place that will value you.

- If your boss won't budge, get another job offer. Having two companies interested in you will give you leverage and options.

Pocket Cash

. . .

*"You've got to save for a rainy day. I'm happy if I got no worries
and no bills to pay."*
—AL SULKA

HOW TO SAVE MONEY

Step 1: Open a new savings account. You should aim to have three to
six months' worth of savings socked away in case of emergency. Choose
an account that carries FDIC insurance, no minimum fees, and, if you
can, at least a 4 percent interest rate.

Step 2: Divert funds. Whenever you receive a paycheck, ask your
bank to automatically transfer 10 percent to your new account.
Chances are, if you never see it, you'll hardly even miss it. And if you
do, well, then learn to make do. Tiny budgetary adjustments—like
making your own coffee at home rather than splurging for a latte every
day, or inflating your tires to get better gas mileage—make a big difference.

Step 3: Revel in your success. Check in on your savings a few times
a year to ensure adequate growth.

More Handy Tips

- If you're planning to start a family, switch careers, travel to Italy,
  or buy a house, open a separate savings account for the venture
  and give it a name that means something to you. For example,

"Money for my honey," "My big chance at my dream job," "Viva Italia!" or "No more couch surfing." That'll help you tap into it for its designated purpose only.

- Charge yourself interest. Vow never to dip into your SOS fund before you deposit the funds, but if you must, require yourself to pay it back, plus 10 percent.

- Hey you, wake up! This money stuff is totally boring but very important. Step it up!

- Every night before jumping into your PJs, empty the pockets of your trousers. Any loose change you find should go into a designated jar. Once the jar is full (and you'll be surprised how quickly it fills up), roll the coins or take the jar to a bank to tally it. Stock this away with your savings, or if you can swing it, designate it as your very own "tip jar" and treat yourself to something fun.

Work Well

• • •

*"People respect you based on your actions and what you do to help others.
Work hard and have good ethics. Then if you have a problem,
you'll always have a friend."*
—ANGEL RODRIGUEZ

HOW TO NAVIGATE OFFICE POLITICS

Step 1: Keep your eyes and ears open. Whether you like it or not, workplaces can often resemble *Survivor* island, minus the torch-snuffing ceremonies. Keep your head down (and mouth shut) and work hard, but also try to understand the relationships around you. Is it coincidence that the new hire has the same last name as the CEO? Probably not. Does everyone play on the company softball team, or is it just the slackers? Which person is revered by all? Know the dynamics of your office. They can help or hinder your career.

Step 2: Stay positive by being stingy with your criticism and generous with your praise. Gossiping, tearing people down, or whining by the watercooler, even if everybody else is doing it, will always come back to haunt you in one way or another. Instead, find common ground with each person and connect. Maybe you'll find other soccer players, or *Parenthood* fans, or Penn Staters. There are so many ways to build relationships. Do some digging and mine that gold. You'll be happier for it.

Step 3: Work it. Once you've built a strong network of allies—and ideally every single person in your office will be your ally—you'll be able to tap into it whenever you need extra support.

More Handy Tips

- Save the drama for your mama. In fact, spare your mama, too. Nobody likes drama. If you see something going down—tongues wagging, people complaining, plots hatching—stay out of it. Forget about the petty stuff, and work toward your own big vision with passion.

- Listen to office gossips, but never participate. They *will* repeat everything you say to someone else.

- As with all relationships, the more you give, the more you get. Always give credit where it's due and support your colleagues when you can. When you share your power, it'll only grow.

Command a Room

• • •

"If you're going to make a speech, make sure you know what you're going to talk about before you get up there. Print it, memorize it, and practice out loud."
—PHILIP SPOONER

HOW TO GIVE A SPEECH

Step 1: Prepare yourself. Know your topic inside and out, and once you've researched and memorized all of your points, do the same for the opposing viewpoint. If you've done your homework, you can take the stage feeling confident in your expertise.

Step 2: Have an opinion. Even if you are incredibly brilliant and interesting—and surely you are—no one wants to hear you talk for the sake of talking. Make a point. Prove something. State your case early on and then build it.

Step 3: Know your audience. While you may make the same argument in your speech anywhere, tailor your jokes and stories to each specific crowd. That means no Lady Gaga references at the retirement home. No Lady Gaga costume at the retirement home, either. Your demeanor and dress should match the audience and occasion.

Step 4: Take notes. If you don't have the luxury of a teleprompter, for goodness' sake, don't write your talking points on your hand. Instead, practice reading your speech word for word. Then transfer it to an outline and practice reading it from that. Once you've got your points polished, transfer them to index cards.

Step 5: Rehearse. Do it until you have your speech down pat and are able to make eye contact throughout. Deliver it in front of the mirror, your Flip camera, your friends, even your dog, if she's a good listener. Practice it in different locations, so that you'll be comfortable anywhere (and won't be surprised on the big day when you're not standing in your bedroom). The more you rehearse, the more natural you'll be in front of a crowd.

More Handy Tips

- Speak to your audience as if you were speaking one-on-one to any person in the audience.

- Don't race through your points. Allow time for them to sink in.

- Use plain language. Unnecessary, highfalutin vocabulary words will only make you sound pretentious, not smart.

- Make eye contact with your audience, but for heaven's sake, don't just stare at one person. That would be so embarrassing for him and you. Move your eyes around the room.

- High school government races, sales pitches, and presidential elections have been won—and lost—based upon the ability to give a good speech. Being a good public speaker can alter your entire career. If you, like most people, fear public speaking, you may find help from Toastmasters International or another local group where folks get together to practice.

- Never tap a microphone and say, "Is this thing on?" or "Check 1–2, check 1–2." Just start talking, and you'll find out soon enough.

Aim High

• • •

"The benefit of setting goals and achieving them is getting that feeling. To strike out somebody, to drive in a run, to kick a field goal, that feeling you get is better than any high you can get from any drug. That's about having a goal, having something set in front of you, and searching for it and reaching for it and having it happen. It's unimaginable."
—BOB KELLY

HOW TO SET GOALS

Step 1: Put them in ink. Grab a pen and paper and write down your long-term dreams, however you define *long-term*. (Depending on your outlook, that may mean ten years from now or ten weeks from now.) And be specific. Rather than say, "I want to be powerful," say "I want to own my own business." Or rather than "I want to look great naked," try "I want to lose ten pounds this summer."

Step 2: Make an action plan. Now that you know your long-term goal, write down your short-term goals, or what you need to do today, this week, this month, or this year to achieve your dream. Set yourself up for success by being realistic and starting small. Let's say your goal is to lose ten pounds this summer (not that you need to, Muscles Malone, but it's just an easy example). You might jot down: "Today: Find my sneakers. This weekend: Walk two miles a day. Next month: Jog a mile and do twenty-five push-ups every day." The more you succeed early on, the more likely you'll enjoy your journey and stick with it.

Step 3: Reinforce it. As hippie-dippie as this may sound, visualize yourself achieving the goal. Or turn it into your daily mantra. It'll make it that much easier to reach. So if losing weight is your goal, picture yourself running on the beach in your bathing suit, proud of your body and totally carefree. Or whisper to yourself whenever you have a moment, "I will lose ten pounds this summer." If someone hears you, and asks "Wha—?" cover yourself. Say, "Oh, It's a lovely day, and feels like summer."

Step 4: Enjoy the process. Frame your goal positively by thinking of it as something you get to do, not something you have to do. Don't think, *I can't sit on my couch and eat a pizza while watching reruns of* The Office. Instead, think, *I get to run four miles tonight.* Awesome!

More Handy Tips

- Set goals based on what you want for yourself, not what others want for you.

- Take counsel from your friends and mentors, but never let others talk you out of your dreams. Believe in yourself, and trust yourself first.

Go Places

. . .

"Oh, I remember my first car. It was a 1947 Buick super convertible. I walked in the dealership with cash in my pocket. The showman told me how much he wanted. I told him how much I'd pay, and I pulled these hundred-dollar bills out of my pocket, set them on the table, and said take it or leave it. I had all the girls chasing my car down the street. I thought they were chasing me!"
—BILL HOLLOMAN

HOW TO BUY A CAR

Step 1: Determine the right car for you. First, consider your budget. Not only will you have to pay for the car, but you'll also have to pony up for the insurance, gas money, any future repairs, and any parking fees. (Your wheels should never cost you more than 10 percent of your take-home pay.) Then consider what you'll use it for. If you plan on using it to go hiking in the mountains every weekend or to drop your three kids off at school every day, a little red Corvette doesn't sound like the right fit. Likewise, if you plan on just driving short distances in your sunny, warm neighborhood, you probably don't need a huge gas-guzzling SUV. Your wants may be different from your needs, but you've got to address your needs first.

Step 2: Get educated. Whether you're buying your car new or used, it's important to know the going prices. Luckily, thanks to the Internet, you no longer have to subject yourself to a dealer's tap-dancing to get some real numbers. Just check the local dealers' going prices at Edmunds (www.edmunds.com) or Kelley Blue Book (www.kbb.com), or call or email them directly. However you get in touch, state the year, make, model, miles, condition, and warranty of the car you're interested in, and ask for the going price. You'll get a sneak peak at not only the price tag of the car, but also the personality of the seller. Buy only from someone who makes you feel comfortable. If a salesman insults you, intimidates you, or condescends to you, don't give him your business.

Step 3: Take a test drive. Once you've chosen a car you like, take it out for a spin, and drive it more like Mario Andretti than your old uncle Mario. Really put the car through its paces. Hit bumps, climb hills, take sharp curves, drive fast on the highway, and test the brakes on the side streets. Don't forget to try all the bells and whistles (sunroof, radio, heated seats), too, before returning the car to the dealer. Then, however much you love this set of wheels, keep it to yourself, hand over the keys, thank the seller, and walk away. Test-drive more cars, if you want.

Step 4: Negotiate a deal. Once you know exactly the car you want, call around and get a real price from three dealers, letting each one know that you're ready to buy and are shopping around. Then leverage whatever power you've got. Do you have competing offers? Do you have five kids and plan on buying them all cars when they turn sixteen? Do you have the luxury of waiting for a year-end special instead? Be nice but firm, and don't get suckered into paying for things you don't want or need.

Step 5: Seal the deal, always knowing you can walk away at any moment. You've got to be equally prepared to do either.

More Handy Tips

- The best time to buy a car is on the last Monday or Tuesday of the month. Not only will the lot likely be less crowded, giving you the salesman's undivided attention, but many salesmen try to meet a monthly sales quota to earn a bonus. If they're short, you might get a better deal.

- Before buying any used car, get the vehicle's history at www.car fax.com, if the dealer hasn't already done it for you. It costs thirty-five bucks, but it'll tell you if it's ever been in any major accidents.

- Be as flexible as you can on the extras, and you'll be more likely to get a better price.

- If you don't have the bucks to buy a car right now, consider leasing one instead.

- Always trust your gut.

Find Shelter
· · ·
"Don't buy a house on the bank of a river."
—Frank Walter

How to Buy a House

Step 1: Assess whether you're ready. It's a good time to buy a house if you have money in the bank (ideally, 20 percent of the purchase price, plus six months' of savings), more money coming in steadily, good credit, and a mind to stick around town for a while. If you're on the fence about any of these, there's no shame in renting. After all, there is something to be said for flexibility and the ability to call the landlord when something breaks.

Step 2: Know what you need. Write down everything you require in a new home, including the location, size of the property, amenities, and condition. Consider the school district if you have kids, your commute to work, the air quality, crime rates, taxes, storage, and outdoor maintenance. No matter how passionately you feel about it, a pool with a waterfall and a wet bar are not necessities. You can always install those things later.

Step 3: Get preapproved for a home loan. Find a mortgage broker, who can compare rates at various banks to find you the best deal, and get a letter stating how much the bank will allow you to borrow when the time comes. If you do find a house you love, and other parties are interested in it, too, you can wave this letter in the air like you just don't care and the seller will know that you, above all others, actually have the financial power to do the deal. Point: you. Other guy: zero.

Step 4: Go hunting. Check the classifieds, scour the Internet, and put out an all-points bulletin with a broker, who will be able to show you properties on the market that will hopefully fit your needs. Just remember, brokers work for the seller, not you, so tell them what you're looking for in a home and your price range, but keep your money cards close to your chest. However you do it, look at as many homes as you can, until you find one you love—and can afford.

Step 5: Make an offer. Once you've found a property you want, ask your Realtor or check Trulia (www.trulia.com) or Zillow (www.zillow.com) for comps, or prices that similar, nearby houses have sold for recently. Knowing what others have paid will help you get a sense of whether the seller's asking price is too high (or, in rare cases, too low). When you've decided how much you'd like to offer, call the broker (or owner, if it's for sale by owner) and submit your offer. He may or may not accept it, at which point you can either close the deal or make a counteroffer.

Step 6: Prep the deal. Once you've agreed on a price, the house goes "in contract" while you take care of business. Hire a home inspector, who will check the property for any major problems. (If some arise, the seller may decide to, or in some cases be required to, fix them before proceeding with the sale.) Finalize your loan. Line up your homeowner's insurance, and then set your closing date.

Step 7: Close the deal. Once everything is in order, you'll meet the seller, along with a bazillion other people (lenders, lawyers, and title companies), to transfer the title, pay transfer taxes, and receive the keys.

Step 8: Pop a bottle of bubbly. Congrats on your new home!

More Handy Tips

- Before applying for a mortgage, make sure your credit is in good shape. Pay every debt in full and on time.

- When you finalize your mortgage, add a rider to your contract that states that if the interest rates go down before closing, your bank will offer you the better rate.

- Bring a digital camera with you while you're house hunting, and take notes on each property so you can remember the pros and cons.

- Just because a bank will loan you an exorbitant amount of money doesn't mean you should actually borrow that much. Stay within your comfort zone, and spend no more than 28 percent of your gross monthly income on your mortgage payment, insurance, and taxes.

- Schedule one final walk-through of the home before the closing to make sure everything looks good.

Set Your Terms

· · ·

*"I always thought a bargain was where both parties were satisfied in the end.
Not that I got the best of you or you got the best of me."*
—CHUCK TATUM

HOW TO NEGOTIATE A BETTER DEAL

Step 1: Work up your courage. You'll never get a discount if you don't ask for one. Almost everything is on sale, if you know how to haggle.

Step 2: Know the market. Be realistic about the price you want. If every butcher is selling the same cut for six to eight dollars a pop, don't expect to buy one for a dollar. But do ask your seller to match the lowest price. If you're buying more than one, ask for a bigger break.

Step 3: Know your audience. You'll be more likely to get discounts at locally owned stores rather than multinational chains and from managers rather than clerks. If you're dealing with someone who can't offer you a discount, kindly ask to speak with his superior. Be charming, if you can. Nobody wants to go the extra mile for a horse's ass.

Step 4: Look for flaws. This may feel a bit shady, but it really isn't. Examine the item you'd like to buy for any imperfections. If it's got any stains, scratches, pulls, or dents, you'll be more likely to get an automatic damaged-good discount, which is usually at least 10 percent.

Step 5: Offer to pay in cash. Stores have to pay a small fee to credit card companies if you use plastic. By paying in cash, they'll likely pass that savings on to you, if you ask for it.

Step 6: Walk away. Sometimes the threat of losing the sale is enough to make the seller cave. If he doesn't, just keep on walking. You've already determined that the price is not right.

More Handy Tips

- Be firm. Serious hagglers actually get better deals than sweet ones. When you get down to the nitty-gritty deal making, try not to smile, stammer, or blush.

- Be friendly. Insulting the seller or his products won't make him want to do you any favors.

Keep Your Shirt

• • •

"A bet is fun if winning is neat and losing doesn't hurt. Wager a chocolate milk shake after a game. It's a great thing."
—BOB KELLY

HOW TO MAKE A FRIENDLY WAGER

Step 1: Make the invitation. Find a willing and honest friend, and propose a bet on the event of your choosing (who can run to the tree faster, who can hit the green in one stroke on a par three, or who will win the Super Bowl). Agree on the parameters before proceeding.

Step 2: Set the stakes. Only ever bet what you can afford—and are fully prepared—to lose. Even if the odds are in your favor and you're confident that you'll win, you must remember that gambling is *always* chancy. When placing your wager, consider your risk more heavily than your reward.

Step 3: Shake on it. Once you've each agreed on the rules and stakes, then look your friend in the eye and grasp hands to make it official. If you'd like, you can even seal the deal verbally by adding "It's a bet" or "We're on." If you really want to make your opponent nervous, throw back your head and belly-laugh.

Step 4: Watch and wait. Using good sportsman-like conduct (see page 164), allow whatever event you just bet on to transpire. You may cheer on your contender (even if it's you), but do be gracious enough to refrain from trash-talking your opponent. It's just bad form.

Step 5: Reconcile your bet. Regardless of the stakes you set, remember that you've already put something even more valuable on the line: your reputation. If you've lost, pay up and offer the winner another handshake and even a few kind words, if you can muster them. If you've won, collect your winnings and thank your worthy opponent.

More Handy Tips

- Bet for fun, not to prove a point. There is a difference between making a friendly wager once in a while and being a know-it-all who just wants to be right. If you find yourself often saying, "Oh, yeah? Wanna bet?"—stop talking and listen. If you don't, odds are you won't have too many friends after a while.

- Before wagering any money, always consider the gentleman's bet. The winner receives respect and satisfaction, while the loser must endure the shame of choosing poorly.

- Gamble only in moderation. Placing bets once in a while is perfectly fine, but if you find yourself obsessing over your wagers, taking too many risks, or losing sleep over your habit, seek help at www.gamblersanonymous.org.

5

Thriving

. . .

*Practice good health every day, and you'll live longer and
be happier. It's that simple.*

Get Smooth

. . .

"I have such tender skin. After I shave, I put on the aftershave. It smells so good. Then I walk over to my wife, I lean over her, and I rub my cheek against her face on each side. Then I sneak in a little smooch. That's the routine every time I shave. I know if I keep shaving, I can keep rubbing cheeks with her."

—JOE TOTH

HOW TO GET THE PERFECT SHAVE

Step 1: Wake yourself up. You're about to put something very sharp on something that is, no doubt, very handsome, so you should at least be conscious while doing it. Have a strong cup of coffee (see page 232 for instructions) and read the paper while stroking your chin and pretending your whiskers make you look like George Clooney. Once your eyes are fully open and your blood is pumping, proceed to the next step.

Step 2: Steam your face. Hot water opens your pores and softens your whiskers, so either take a long, hot shower or lay a steaming, wet towel on your mug for a few minutes. Ah, that feels good, doesn't it?

Step 3: Prep your beard. A proper shave will leave your cheeks feeling as soft as a baby's bottom (that's a good thing), and to do it right, you've got to massage in a few drops of pre-shave oil before lathering up. It'll help your razor cut your whiskers, not your skin.

Step 4: Lather up. Wet a badger-hair shaving brush and use it to work your shaving soap or cream into a thick, frenzied lather. Then apply a thin layer to your cheeks, chin, lip area, and neck. Work your brush in a circular motion on your face to help your whiskers stand on end.

Step 5: Shave with the grain. Using long even strokes and starting at your sideburns, draw your razor along the grain of your hair. Going with your whisker traffic helps prevent razor burn and ingrown hairs. You'll get most, but not all, of your scruff, but don't worry your pretty face about that. You'll take a second pass soon.

Step 6: Lather again. Be speedy. You're a pro at this by now.

Step 7: Shave across the grain. Clean up any rough patches, drawing your razor across any stubborn whiskers.

Step 8: Splash with cold water. The icier, the better. Cold water not only cleans your face but also closes your pores. Dab dry with a clean towel.

Step 9: Soothe your skin. A few pats of alcohol-free aftershave should do the trick. Remember, your goal is to moisturize your weary skin, not to give off a fragrance that wafts so heavily in the wind that it'll disorient nearby birds.

More Handy Tips

- Always use a sharp razor. Using a dull one is just asking for trouble.

- Use shaving soap or cream, rather than those airy shaving foams. They protect your skin from nicks better.

- If you have sensitive skin, allow your shaving cream to sit on your face for a minute or two before you take your razor to it, and leave your neck, which often has the grizzliest hair, for last. Doing so will help soften up the whiskers even more.

- When shaving your upper lip, curl it over your upper teeth to help pull the skin taut and avoid cuts.

- If you make a mistake, dab the nick with a styptic pencil to prevent yourself from gushing blood.

Go Grizzly

• • •

"The first time I grew a beard was in college. Two other guys and I got in my '48 Studebaker and drove to Alaska on a dirt highway to get a high-paying construction job. We got there a week late, and the only jobs we could get were as gandy dancers on the railroad, pulling out old ties and driving spikes. I grew a great beard. I thought I looked great. I felt more manly."
—Buck Buchanan

HOW TO GROW A BEARD

Step 1: Make a vow now. The most difficult part of growing a rug on your face is enduring that awkward phase between being clean-shaven and realizing your full Paul Bunyan potential. It takes a good, solid four to six weeks to get to the point where you'll look decent. Put your razor under lock and key and only reach for it in case of absolute emergency (say, your boss threatens to fire you, or your sweetie threatens to never kiss you again).

Step 2: Prepare some comebacks. During the growth phase, everyone (and his mother) will act as if their eyes have fallen out of their heads and ask you, incredulously, "Are you growing a beard?" The accent may be on the "*you*," implying that you're not man enough to have facial hair, or on "*beard,*" implying that you're not crazy enough to have facial hair. Don't be swayed by their comments. Simply rub your whiskers and say, "Don't make me sic my big blue ox on you."

Step 3: Monitor the patterns. Due to circumstances beyond his control, not every man is blessed with perfectly even facial hair. As your whiskers grow in, you may notice a few areas on your face where the hair is thinner or nonexistent. Dems the breaks. If your cheeks are bald, opt for a goatee instead. If your chin is hairless, how about a biker 'stache? No lip hair? Try an Amish-style beard, son.

Step 4: Shape your beard. After four to six weeks have passed and you're rocking your Paul Bunyan, reclaim your razor and shape your neckline. Draw an imaginary line about an inch above your Adam's apple, angled slightly upward to meet the hairline on the back of your neck. Shave anything below that line. Unless your beard is obstructing your vision or someone mistakes you for Chewbacca, your cheeks are probably all right as they are.

Step 5: Groom it. Shampoo and condition your facial hair just as you do the hair to the north, or, if you want to get fancy, use a special beard wash. Then comb it every day and trim it once or twice a week with a beard trimmer to avoid being mistaken for one of the ZZ Top guys.

More Handy Tips

- Check your beard after any meal or snack. There's nothing more off-putting than looking at a guy with potato chips or arugula suspended in his facial hair.

- Start your beard on vacation. Not only do you not have to worry about packing your shaving kit, but you won't be bothered by people asking you what you're doing.

- Consider growing one for winter. It'll help protect your face from the wind and chill.

- When your skin gets itchy—and, oh, it will at first—calm it with moisturizer.

- Beards are great ways to reinvent yourself. Al Gore grew one after losing the 2000 Supreme Court decision, and he went on to win a Nobel Peace Prize and an Academy Award. Imagine what you can do with some facial hair!

Curl Up

• • •

"When I graduated from flight school, I grew my mustache. It made me look like [actor] Robert Taylor. The ladies were falling all over themselves for him, and I didn't have good looks, so I thought I'd go the next route."
—Bill Holloman

HOW TO WAX A MUSTACHE

Step 1: Buy some wax, matching its color to the color of your 'stache. If you're just shaping the ends of your mustache, a soft wax will do. If the whole thing is growing into your mouth and you're starting to look like a walrus, first of all, ew! Second of all, opt for a stiff wax to strongly encourage your lip hair to grow sideways.

Step 2: Dab it on. Squeeze a smidge on your finger and smooth it on your mustache, starting just beneath your nose and working your way out to the sides. Add more wax, as needed.

Step 3: Comb it out. Using a very fine-tooth comb, work your wax through your mustache from the center outward so the hair above your lip is parallel, not perpendicular, to your lip. Wait a few minutes for your wax to set before proceeding to step 4.

Step 4: Curl the ends. Once you've gotten the wax all the way to the ends of your mustache and it's just beginning to stiffen up, pinch your hair together and, if you'd like, gently twist it. Then shape the ends as you desire. Pull them straight up to go for the Salvador Dalí look. Wrap them tightly around a pencil (and then, of course, remove the pencil) to look like Snidely Whiplash, the villain on *The Rocky and Bullwinkle Show.* Or channel President Taft and gently guide them into an elegant swoosh.

More Handy Tips

- If you're using a stiff wax, it helps to warm it between your index finger and thumb before applying.

- If your mustache is short except for the very ends, you may wax just the ends.

- Refrain from winding the ends of your mustache between your fingers all day. You'll not only annoy the people around you but also weaken your hair, putting your hard-earned handlebar in jeopardy.

Look Trim

• • •

"A good barber is one who does a good job that leaves you satisfied. After a while, he'll remember your cut and proceed to do it the same way it's always done. The conversation? That's just to pass the time."

—Joe Babin

How to Get a Haircut

Step 1: Find a good, old-fashioned barber, who can wield his clippers as nimbly as scissors and who will charge reasonably for it. If you're too shy to ask a friend (or any handsome stranger) where he goes for a cut, then look for that telltale striped pole on the street, stake out the shop, and take a few minutes to watch who comes and goes. Are the "afters" better than the "befores"? Is the joint hopping, or does the barber look bored? You want a friendly, busy, neatly dressed barber, not a loner with no customers or a slob who pays little attention to detail.

Step 2: Give good instructions. Once you hop in the chair, be clear about what you want. Tell him how much you'd like off the sides and top, where you like your part, whether or not you'd like any layers, and what you'd like to do with your sideburns and the back. (Unless you're getting a buzz cut, ask him to follow the natural hairline on your neck; get it squared off only if you're going supershort.) He may do it on his own, but if he doesn't, ask him to snip off any stragglers from your ears and eyebrows. Your ears should be bald, and your eyebrows should lie flat. If you can braid the hair on either, it's too long.

Step 3: Shoot the breeze. Getting a haircut at a barbershop is as much of a social outing as it is a grooming ritual. Make conversation. The game, the local news, your or his family are all within bounds. Steer clear of politics or religion, unless you already know that you agree. After all, he's wielding the snippers, which gives him the power to make you look like a stud or dweeb. You don't want to tick him off.

Step 4: Check his progress. Don't wait until the end of the cut to look at what he's doing. He wants to make you happy, so you'll be a repeat customer. Set him up for success by speaking up and telling him whether you'd like a little more or a little less off as he works.

Step 5: Pay up. Hand over his fee, plus a 15 to 20 percent tip if you were happy with the experience. Look him in the eye to thank him, and shake hands before you leave. He'll be more likely to remember you, and your cut, when you return.

Step 6: Repeat as necessary. You'll probably need a cut at least every four to six weeks. If you were happy with his work, go back to your same guy and ask for the usual. Before you know it, you'll be buds.

More Handy Tips

- Some barbers will also give shaves. It sounds a little terrifying to have another man drag a straight razor along your throat, but do it at least once in your life. You won't be sorry.

- If you know exactly what style you'd like, bring in a picture. If you tell him you want a Don Draper or a cut like the teacher on *Glee*, he'll likely have no idea what you're talking about. Make it easy for him.

Drive 'em Wild

• • •

"I love cologne! Of course, expensive cologne is better than cheap cologne. I put a lot on, and I feel good, but my wife doesn't like when I wear too much. She waves her hands in front of her nose."
—Angel Rodriguez

How to Wear Cologne

Step 1: Understand the purpose. You know how when your uncle Vernon comes to visit you he calls when he's getting close to alert you of his impending arrival? Well, your cologne should not serve the same purpose in your life, announcing your arrival fifteen minutes ahead of time. Unless another person is standing close enough to kiss you, he or she should not be able tell that you're wearing any scent at all.

Step 2: Choose your scent. Go for something fresher and lighter for the daytime. Reserve the muskier, hot 'n' heavy scents for nighttime. And make sure your cologne doesn't clash with whatever you've already got on, like your deodorant, aftershave, body soap, or shampoo.

Step 3: Put it on. Whether you spritz it or dab it, put a touch on your neck and some on the inside of each wrist. When it doubt, use less than you think you should. Way less.

More Handy Tips

- Heat amplifies scents, so go even easier on hot days.

- If the people around you start sneezing or complaining of head-aches, you've got too much on. Go quietly rinse off, before return-ing to the party.

- Cologne doesn't last forever. If you've owned yours so long that you can no longer read the words on the bottle or it has turned an altogether different color, it's time to replace it.

- Cologne should never replace a shower or a good toothbrushing.

- Never put cologne where the sun don't shine. It may sound like a good idea, but it sure won't feel like one.

Be Proud

· · ·

"Prepare yourself. Educate yourself. That's the most important thing. People want to start at the top, and they don't know how to climb the ladder. When the door is open, you've got to be ready to walk through."

—BILL HOLLOMAN

HOW TO FIND SELF-CONFIDENCE

Step 1: Be your own best friend. Yes, this sounds totally, ridiculously, eye-rollingly hokey, but here's the point: You'd never ever let anyone else tear down your best friend the way you probably tear down yourself. Why the double standard? Treat that little troll inside your head who always seems to rip you whenever you're feeling unsure of yourself the same way you'd treat him if he were ripping on your best bud. Tell him to shove it. You've got better things to do than listen to him.

Step 2: Keep your chin up. Literally. And throw your shoulders back, and stand tall. Not only does your posture send a message to everyone around you, but it also sends one to your own brain. Own your space. You've only got one shot at this world. Don't waste it.

Step 3: Sweat. Strong muscles might help you feel better about yourself, but those feel-good endorphins that course through your bloodstream while you exercise definitely will. Whether you like it or not, you will be in a better mood and feel better about yourself after you do something physical. Go run, chop wood, anything that gets your heart pounding.

Step 4: Set goals. They don't even have to be big ones, like winning the presidency or competing in a marathon. Try achievable day-to-day ones for starters, striking up a conversation with a neighbor or learning something new, like planting a tree (page 3) or playing the harmonica (page 255). The more successes you rack up, the more confident you'll begin to feel.

Step 5: Fake it until you make it. You may be quaking inside at the thought of asking your boss for a raise or asking a cutie-pie for a date. Pretend, even for just those ten seconds or ten minutes, that you have no fear, and others will start treating you accordingly—as if you can do anything. And you know what? Soon enough, you'll be able to.

More Handy Tips

- Don't confuse arrogance with confidence. Of the two, only one will burn you in the end.

- A pair of clean undies and a decent shirt can do wonders for the mind. Get out of your sweats and dress like you're ready to lead the world, not like you're ready to lie on the couch.

- If you find yourself in a funk, get out of your own head and start helping others. Volunteer. Tutor. Clean your park. You'll be amazed at what you can accomplish.

Stay Cool

. . .

"There's no question that I have a temper, but it must not be at the top of my head, because I've very seldom been that angry. The few times in my life I did lose it, I got angry with myself afterward. To lose control of yourself is a stupid thing to do."

—Joe Babin

How to Control your Temper

Step 1: Chill out. It's healthy to get angry sometimes, but if you find yourself filled with rage or tempted to hurt, physically or emotionally, the people around you, check yourself. Before doing something you will no doubt regret, take a deep breath and count to ten. If that doesn't release some steam, remove yourself from the situation. Take a walk (or run), go to your room and shut the door, head to the movie theater for whatever's playing, or crack open a notebook and get your feelings on paper.

Step 2: Express yourself. Sometimes you'll find that stepping away from the situation helps give you perspective. Once you've figured out what it is exactly that made you so angry, calmly and rationally explain that to the person who upset you. Even though you may be tempted to rattle off a list of all the ways this person wronged you throughout history, stick only to the issue at hand. And rather than talk about what he did, talk about how you feel. Making accusations won't help you, since your goal is to extinguish your anger, not fuel it.

Step 3: Find solutions. Work together to find a resolution that suits you both. If it's an apology you need, just ask for it.

More Handy Tips

- Whenever you feel your blood pressure start to spike, try visualizing yourself in a calm and peaceful place. It sounds a little dippy, but it does work.

- Practice forgiveness. Holding a grudge only infects your own heart and head with negative thoughts. Letting go of your anger doesn't mean you're excusing the other person's misdeed. It just means you're making room for yourself to heal.

Do It

...

"I think inner strength has to be built in. You can't rent it. No one can tell you how to get it. It's an inner feeling of being a survivor and surviving. I think all people have it, but some people exercise it more than others."
—CHUCK TATUM

HOW TO FIND SELF-DISCIPLINE

Step 1: Take control. Sure, some of what happens to you in life is beyond your power, but all the other stuff? Yep, it's on you, buddy. It is your life, after all. Your dreams. So, either chase them with all your might, or let 'em slip away. Take responsibility for your own life.

Step 2: Change your mind. You have to think of self-discipline as things you *get* to do for yourself, not things you *have* to do. Otherwise, it's just a drag. So think, *I get to build muscle today* (and pound your chest), not, *Aw, I hafta go to the gym again. Poor me* (snivel). Think, *I get to knock their socks off at work today* (and wink at yourself in the mirror), not, *Poor me, I hafta be there eight more hours* (and pick your nose).

Step 3: Know what you want. For example, if you want to get a raise, you sometimes have to skip after-work drinks with your buddies in order to put in a few extra hours at the office. That's discipline. If you want to win the game, you need to go to bed an hour or two earlier the night before rather than staying up late playing Mortal Kombat. That's discipline. If you want to write a bestselling novel, you will have to sit alone at your computer and write, rather than hang out with your pals at a coffee shop, jawing about how great your book will be. That's discipline. To find it, you've got to know yourself and think big picture. Getting a raise isn't just about dollars and cents; it's about power and security. Winning a game isn't just about victory; it's about strength and confidence. Once you figure out what you really want, you'll be better equipped to go after it.

Step 4: Set small goals—and meet them. Summoning your willpower will get easier and easier every time you do it successfully, so make it easy on yourself from the get-go. Set small, realistic, daily or weekly goals that get you pointing in the right direction. Write them down, even, and cross them off. Once you achieve your little goals, it'll be easier to keep going. You successes will become part of who you are.

Step 5: Reward yourself. Check in on your goals regularly and see how you're doing. If you slipped up, try again. If you achieved them, treat yourself in some way. You want to feel proud of your accomplishments. Plus, all work and no play makes Jack a dull boy, right?

More Handy Tips

- Ask your friends for help if you need it, but don't ask for their approval. Self-discipline comes from what's inside you, not what's inside them.

- If you slip, that's okay. Everybody has moments of weakness, and it doesn't mean you're a failure. Just don't give up. You only fail if you quit trying. Next time will be easier.

6

Bonding

. . .

You have to be a friend to have a friend.

Get a Grip

...

"A good handshake is important. It's the sincerity of it that matters. If I shake hands with a man and his hand is limp, I think of a saying I learned: 'Indifference is the opposite of love.' A limp handshake is an expression of indifference. I'm not impressed by that person."
—BUCK BUCHANAN

HOW TO SHAKE HANDS

Step 1: Greet the person. Approach him head-on, smile, and say hi before extending your hand. Otherwise, he may not see or hear you and you could be left hanging. Embarrassing!

Step 2: Extend your right hand, palm open, thumb pointing up. In this most symbolic of gestures, you're offering your friendship by meeting in the middle.

Step 3: Get a grip. Once you grasp hands, palm-to-palm, thumb-to-thumb, wrap your fingers around his hand firmly, look him in the eye, and shake once or twice.

More Handy Tips

- If you want to convey extreme warmth or empathy, add your left hand to the shake by placing it on top of your friend's hand or on his arm.

- Eye contact is so important. If you can't look your acquaintance in the eye, he'll think you're sketchy. And if he can't look you in the eye, don't trust him.

- A handshake is a sign of friendship, not domination. Be confident in your grip, but don't try to break the bones in your pal's hand. Shake hands as you live: gentle, firm, and true.

Meet Up

. . .

"Every one of us has a sign on our chest. It's invisible but always there. It says, MAKE ME FEEL SPECIAL. If you do that, if you make each person around you feel special, you'll be successful."
—Frank Walter

How to Introduce People

Step 1: Figure out who has the higher rank or level of authority. You've got all of a split second to make your choice, so don't dilly-dally. Your boss, for example, trumps your buddy. Your lover trumps your neighbor. If it's unclear, pick whoever is older.

Step 2: Name the more distinguished party, and present to him the underparty. Include any relevant information he might like to know. "Mr. President, may I present Ward Cleaver, my neighbor." You can also substitute "have you met" for "may I present." On less formal occasions, feel free to simply say both parties' names back-to-back. "David Starsky, Ken Hutchinson."

Step 3: You're finished! No need to do the reverse introduction or repeat names. Your peeps already have all they need to know.

More Handy Tips

- If you're introducing one person to a group, address the person closest to you and present the newcomer to her. Then move around the group, simply naming each of the members.

- Try to avoid making statements such as "You must meet" or "Please shake hands with." No one likes being told what to do.

- If there's a strained silence after you make the introduction, help your friends along by letting them know what they have in common—but keep it flattering. Rather than "Harry, have you met Ron? I think you both went through very awkward teenage years." Say, "Harry, have you met Ron? I think you both went to the same school."

Pal Around

• • •

"No man is meant to be an island. What is life other than living and getting along with your friends and appreciating your friends and their successes and being with them when they need help? What's the sense of living if you aren't doing that?"
—BOB KELLY

HOW TO BE A GOOD FRIEND

Step 1: Be true to yourself. It doesn't make sense to radically change who you are in order to get someone else to like you. If you're a liberal, don't don your Revolutionary War costume and expect to find your best mate at a Tea Party. If you're a folksinger, don't deck yourself out in Ed Hardy and head to the Jersey Shore. Instead, get to know (and love) who you are, and be a good friend to yourself first.

Step 2: Keep your word. If you tell your friend you'll be somewhere, be there. Honor your commitments, even if something supposedly better comes along. After all, if you can't count on your friends, who can you count on?

Step 3: Earn trust. If your friend confides in you, keep it to yourself (unless his safety is at stake). If someone is dissing him, have his back. And never, under any circumstances, make your friend look or feel bad in front of others, even if you're just joking. Loyal friends champion and protect one another.

Step 4: Make time. Be the first to call. Help out as much as you can. And don't keep score of who did (or didn't do) what for whom. In friendship, the more you give, the more you get.

Step 5: Try to understand. There will be times in life when your friend gets distracted, say, by a new job, a new love, a new baby, or a new motorcycle, and spends less time with you. Don't begrudge him the other things in his life, especially if they are making him happy. Trust that your pal will come back around, and when he does, welcome him easily.

More Handy Tips

- If you find yourself talking more than you're listening, shut your mouth and open your ears.

- Loners are cool in the movies, but in real life they're just, well, often lonely. If you find yourself in a new city, job, or stage of life, and realize you're standing alone, concentrate on being the sort of guy who is a good friend. Friends will soon follow.

- You may have many acquaintances, but true friends are rare. If you find one, invest in the relationship, and it'll reward you for a lifetime.

Jump In

· · ·

"It takes a little bit of nerve every once in a while. When you see your chance, do it. If someone needs a player, just go. But if both teams are full, you're banging your head against the door."
—Bob Kelly

How to Join a Pickup Game

Step 1: Come ready to play. If you know of a particular court or field where games spontaneously happen, show up dressed and ready for action. Bring your own ball, too. Either it'll be your ticket in, or—if they already have one—you can use it to entertain yourself on the sidelines (and show off your skills) until it's time to jump in.

Step 2: Engage. Longing looks won't get you on the team. Speak up and ask the captain (or whoever looks friendliest) if anyone needs another player.

Step 3: Wait around. Oftentimes, a team will need a sub if another player gets pooped, injured, or called home early. Seize the moment. Ask the departing player if you can take his spot, announce the roster change, and then hit the field!

More Handy Tips

- The more eager you are to play, the more likely it is you'll get to. Don't stand on the sidelines, texting your friends. Instead, cheer good plays and be ready to grab the ball if it goes out of bounds.

- If at first you don't succeed, come back tomorrow (a little earlier, this time) and try again.

Circle Up

...

"It's very hard to ask for help. A good deal of independence is well worthwhile, but if you have someone who you know or suspect can give you help or advice, you're not being fair to yourself if you don't take it."
—Frank Walter

How to Ask for Help

Step 1: Speak up. If you're feeling overwhelmed, don't suffer in silence. Instead, hold your head high, take a deep breath, and reach out to someone you trust. It may be difficult to do, but opening up to a friend will make you feel supported and her feel valued. It's a win–win situation.

Step 2: Be specific about your needs. Do you require sympathy, guidance, or action? You'll be more likely to get what you need if you ask for it directly.

Step 3: Say thanks. Let your buddy know you'll return the favor anytime.

Step 4: Feel proud. By seeking help, you've not only come closer to solving your problem, but you've also demonstrated tremendous resourcefulness and bravery. Pound your chest a few times, or pump your fist in the air. You rock!

More Handy Tips

- If you're really struggling, try helping someone else. Not only will you feel instantly empowered, but you'll also gain confidence in your own problem-solving abilities.

- Don't look for a quick fix (or all the answers) from your confidant. Know that the most he can do is guide you toward change—you'll have to do the rest yourself.

Stay Mum

· · ·

*"I'm a professional bitcher. I've opened my mouth sometimes when
I shouldn't have and I'm sorry about it. But other times, I wish
I'd said more."*
—PHILIP SPOONER

HOW TO KNOW WHEN TO KEEP QUIET

Step 1: Judge your words. If you don't have anything nice to say, you know what to do. Same goes for if you don't have anything interesting to add to the conversation. Talking just to hear yourself talk or to have all eyes on you is not a good enough excuse to open your piehole, especially if you have no knowledge of the subject matter. You'll only annoy those around you, and make yourself look like a fool.

Step 2: Keep secrets. Gossips usually spill the beans for one of two reasons: They either want to make themselves feel special by being in the know, or they want to cash in on a secret in order to forge a relationship with the listener. Both excuses are terribly lousy. There are better ways to feel good and make friends than to sell someone else out. Besides, your listener will eventually forget the secret you told, but will always remember that you told it. Never talk behind someone's back.

Step 3: Learn. If the conversation has gone over your head or you're jumping in late, listen to see what you can absorb. No one will know you're out of your depth unless you show them. By keeping quiet or asking questions, you're giving yourself a chance to catch up.

More Handy Tips

- If you can't keep a secret, don't let anyone tell you one in the first place.

- If you're an expert, don't be afraid to speak up when it's appropriate—but even then, measure your comments. No one likes a know-it-all.

- When in doubt, smile.

Say Sorry

• • •

"Whenever I had something on my mind, I had to get it off my conscience. If I did something I knew my mother wouldn't appreciate, rather than stew, I'd admit up to it right away so I got it off my chest. It's the best way to be. If I ever hurt somebody, I don't know if I could live with that."
—BOB KELLY

HOW TO APOLOGIZE

Step 1: Buck up. Saying sorry is one of the hardest things to do, mostly because doing so is an admission of your mistake. Don't shy away from it. Instead, meet it the same way you'd meet a triumph: head-on.

Step 2: Take responsibility. Think hard about what you did and why you did it without laying the blame on anyone else. Only by taking responsibility for your actions can you guarantee to yourself, and to the person you harmed, that you won't repeat the mistake in the future.

Step 3: Empathize. Put yourself in the other person's shoes. Think even harder about the hurt you caused her and what it felt like, without blaming her for her own pain. Tell the person you understand how much you hurt her and let her know how much you regret what you did.

Step 4: Choose your method. A face-to-face apology is always best. But if you can't because of distance or circumstance, a long letter will do. If you want to be taken seriously, don't apologize by shooting off a quick email or leaving a curt voice mail—neither make it seem like you spent any time thinking about what you did wrong.

Step 5: Promise that it won't happen again. And mean it.

More Handy Tips

- Don't ruin a perfectly good apology with a "but." If you add an excuse or lay blame, you're not taking responsibility for yourself, and your apology loses its worth.

- Create an apology to match the situation. If you bump into an office colleague in the hallway, a simple "Oops, I'm sorry" works wonders. If you've done irreparable damage to someone, a simple "Hey dude, sorry 'bout that!" email won't do.

- Don't say you're sorry unless you mean it. An insincere apology just causes more harm.

Lead the Pack

• • •

"Dogs are loyal. You come home in the evening and, no matter what, they express their joy at having you back."
—Buck Buchanan

How to Teach Your Dog to Sit and Stay

Step 1: Pick a spot. Walk or run your pooch to a quiet place to train. Make sure he has already exercised so he's calm and not yet eaten so he'll be interested in his treats.

Step 2: Motivate him. Hold a treat right in front of his nose. Then slowly move the treat farther up, so that in order to get it he'll have to lean his head back, point his nose up, and lower his hindquarters.

Step 3: Reward him. After he sits, give him the treat, along with a pat on the head and a hearty "Good boy!" If he pops up immediately, repeat step 2. Only give him a treat when his bum is firmly planted on the ground, and only proceed to step 4 when he offers to sit the moment you extend your hand.

Step 4: Repeat steps 1 through 3, saying "Sit" each time. Once he gets the hang of it, praise him each time he sits, but reward him with a treat only every third time. He'll begin to learn that he'll be praised if he sits upon command.

Step 5: Make him stay. After he gets the whole sitting-thing down, instead of rewarding him immediately, command "Stay." Stand still, wait a few beats, and if he remains seated, reward him with a treat.

Step 6: Add duration. Repeat step 5, increasing the amount of time he has to stay with each command. Remember to praise him if he does what you ask.

Step 7: Add distance. Once he understands "Stay," take a step away from him with each subsequent attempt. Eventually, he'll sit and stay, no matter how long you wait or far you walk, until you release him.

More Handy Tips

- Don't get frustrated if your dog doesn't learn immediately. Take the time, make it fun, be consistent, repeat the command, and always provide positive feedback. Stick to it.

- Don't punish your dog for something he hasn't learned or doesn't understand. You're his pack and his leader, so instead take it upon yourself to see that he *does* learn.

- Keep your training sessions short, and master one easy command at a time. Then you can move on to more difficult commands.

- Training with your dog is good for him. It gives him exercise, challenges, and a "job" that keeps him happy.

- Having a well-behaved dog means you can take him more places without worry, and makes for a happier life for you both.

7

Playing

. . .

*The lessons you learn on the field—teamwork, respect,
perseverance—will inform the rest of your life.
Plus, you'll have fun.*

Tee Up

• • •

"I've played golf all my life. Since I was a young boy, I always wanted to be a winner. If I was a winner, I was a hero. I wanted to be a hunk and make an impression on the girls. I wanted to be an excellent performer at anything I tried, and I was always trying!"

—BUCK BUCHANAN

HOW TO DRIVE A GOLF BALL

Step 1: Take a deep breath. Especially if you're hitting off the first hole, all eyes are going to be on you. The people behind are watching to see if you'll slice it, and hold them up all day, and the people in the clubhouse are watching to see if you'll hook it, thus consoling them for their own lousy rounds. Don't let the pressure get to you. Stay loose, keep your head down, and focus on that teeny white ball. And remember, you're here to have fun.

Step 2: Tee up your ball. If you want it to soar higher or you're hitting with the wind, tee it up so the midpoint of the ball sits at the top of the driver's head. If you want it to sail lower or if you're hitting into the wind, tee it up lower.

Step 3: Get a grip. Place your left hand on the handle of the club so the heel of your hand is at the heel of the club, and gently wrap your fingers around it. When you look down, the V that forms between your thumb and index finger should generally be in line with the club. Then add your right hand to your grip the same way, sliding your right hand up until your right pinkie overlaps with your left index finger. If you want to get fancy, you can even interlock your pinkie and pointer.

Step 4: Set yourself up. Approach the ball and stand with your feet slightly wider than hip-width, knees slightly bent, so the ball is lined up with the instep of your left foot and your shoulders and feet are perpendicular to the line you'd like the ball to travel. You're in the right spot if you can draw a straight line between the ball and your left shoulder.

Step 5: Swing back. Keeping your head down, your eye on the ball, and your left arm straight, swing your club back by shifting your weight onto your back foot, turning your hips, and rotating your left shoulder toward your right foot. Your hands should come above your right ear, and your club head should be high in the air, not behind you. After all, it's golf, not baseball.

Step 6: Swing through. Without lifting your head, allow your club to follow its natural arc. As you swing, shift your weight to your front

foot and allow your back foot to pivot after impact. The club will hit the ball at the beginning of your upswing, so be sure to follow through fully.

More Handy Tips

- These instructions are for right-handers. If you're a lefty, switch.

- Physics, not muscle, moves a golf ball. Don't try to power through your swing. Just swing slowly and let the club do the work for you.

- Keep your grip loose. Strangling your club will kill your hands, and your swing.

- Hit the driving range before you hit the fairway to work out any kinks in your stroke.

Go Long

...

"When I was a kid, I didn't have the ten cents to go to the high school football games, so I had to climb a tree and look over the fence. That's tenacity!"
—Chuck Tatum

How to Throw a Perfect Spiral

Step 1: Hold the ball in your dominant hand, cradling the tip between your thumb and index finger, and laying your middle finger, ring finger, and pinkie on the laces. There should be a space between the ball and your palm.

Step 2: Stand with your feet hip-width apart, aiming your weak hip, shoulder, and wrist at your target.

Step 3: Throw the ball. Raise your elbow up to cock the ball right above your ear, shifting your weight to your back foot. Then power through your hips and abs to throw, pointing your hips and belly button toward the target.

Step 4: Make it spiral. Loosen your thumb, snap your wrist, and allow the ball to roll off your fingertips as you release it. Your index finger should be the last one off the ball. When you finish, your throwing hand should meet your opposite hip. You'll know you've done it right if the crowd goes wild.

More Handy Tips

- The spiral comes from your fingertips, but the distance comes from your hips. Throw with force *and* grace.

- Before you throw, hold your weaker hand out in front of you to block tackles or just look cool. Besides, the trophy sculptors will need that image of you to make a bronze replica of your torso.

- As you throw, hold your weak arm tight against your side as your torso rotates. It'll help ensure a solid pass.

- Release the ball sooner for a longer, higher throw. Release it later, and follow through for a shorter pass.

- Get the fundamentals down, so when eleven guys are rushing you, you'll be able to stay calm and get a pass off.

Grease Palms

. . .

"When it rained, I remember, as a boy, there were two things that really worried me. Is my bike outside? And is my glove outside? I couldn't rest until I got them both in. My glove was my life companion."
—BOB KELLY

HOW TO BREAK IN A BASEBALL MITT

Step 1: Soften the leather using your favorite conditioner. Some good options: lanolin (from sheep), neatsfoot oil (from cows), saddle soap, or petroleum jelly. Dab or drizzle just a little bit of it onto a clean, dry cloth. Next, starting in the palm of the mitt and working your way over the entire glove (laces included), gently massage in the oil. Wipe away any excess or your glove will soak up every last bit, making it heavy. If, after this, you feel the urge to kiss your new glove, that's perfectly understandable. Just make sure nobody else sees you.

Step 2: Form the pocket. Toss a baseball or softball into the glove, and then tie your mitt around it, using twine, rope, your shoelaces, or a wire clothes hanger. Let it sit overnight, or for two days, if you can stand it. If you think it'll help, you can even stuff it under your mattress. It might help break it in faster, and it will definitely give you sweet dreams.

Step 3: Play ball. Using your glove is the very best way to make it yours. Head outside with a pal, play catch until the sun sets, and repeat until your glove feels like a natural extension of your hand. You'll never miss a grounder or pop fly again!

More Handy Tips

- Oil your glove whenever it begins to feel dry. Two or three times per season should be plenty.

- In the off-season, when you're not using your glove, tie it up with a ball in the pocket so it maintains its shape.

- In all other areas of life, sharing is wonderful. But not when it comes to a new baseball glove. If you allow someone else to wear it in this early stage, it may form to his hand, not yours. Keep it close.

Sink It

· · ·

"We'd play basketball every day. I scored a hundred points in one game. It's very easy to score. Never miss."

—Al Sulka

How to Shoot a Free Throw

Step 1: Toe the line. Stand with your feet shoulder-width apart, and place your dominant toe on the line directly in front of the basket. Your weaker foot can either be on the same line or slightly behind.

Step 2: Get comfortable with the ball. You've got a full ten seconds to relax into the moment. Do whatever it takes to shake off the pressure, drown out the fans, and focus. Spin the ball, bounce it, take a deep breath, shake your booty, pull your ear, scratch something, whatever chills you out. Once you settle into your own ritual, stick with it for every free throw.

Step 3: Cradle the ball. When you're ready to shoot, hold the ball in your dominant hand, resting it on your fingertips so there's a space between the bottom of the ball and your palm. Use your weaker hand to guide, but not throw, the ball.

Step 4: Shoot. Focusing on the back of the rim and holding the ball just above your forehead, between your eyes, bend your knees. Then, as you power up through your legs, extend your arm toward the basket, allowing the ball to roll off your fingertips for the perfect backspin. Finish on your toes.

More Handy Tips

- Hold the ball so that your fingers are perpendicular, not parallel, to the lines on it. This helps with rotation.

- When shooting, your thumb, pointer, and middle finger will do most of the work. Getting your ring and pinkie fingers too involved could cause chaos and spin the ball sideways.

- To get good ball rotation, point your pointer and middle finger at the basket during your follow-through.

- Practice your free throws every day, as if the game depends on it. It often does!

Stick It

• • •

"We used to play pool for two cents a game, but that was very seldom. It was a rich man's game, because nobody had a pool table."
—AL SULKA

HOW TO SHOOT POOL

Step 1: Line up your shot. Pool is a game of geometry. You need to know angles to sink balls. To figure out your aim, draw an imaginary line from the center of the pocket through the colored ball you'd like to sink. The exact point where your imaginary line emerges from the colored ball is your magic spot. Aim your white cue ball for it, and you'll sink the shot.

Step 2: Grip your stick. Lean over the table with your head directly over the cue and your feet staggered and shoulder-width apart. Wrap your dominant hand around the fat end of the cue so your elbow is pointing north. Next, spread the last three fingers of your weaker hand on the table, a few inches behind the white cue ball, as a base, and loosely wrap your pointer and thumb around the skinny end of the cue stick. Keep your fingers springy and your palm off the table.

Step 3: Shoot. Holding your stick level, take a few slow practice shots, stopping short of the ball. Once you feel confident in your aim, let 'er rip.

More Handy Tips

- To get your cue ball to follow the colored ball, hit it toward the top. To stop it in its tracks, hit it just slightly below center. To get it to roll backward, hit it toward the bottom.

- Know that every pool table is different, depending on the angle of the floor and condition of the felt. Playing on your friend's table with the ripped felt and wobbly leg gives him the "home table" advantage.

- Practice your technique and you'll never miss a shot again. Unless, of course, you're pool sharking. Then miss the first ten until someone challenges you to a bet. Once you've got a taker, sink away. Caution: If you try this, you should also be a very fast runner.

Make Aces

. . .

"I started playing tennis when I was twelve, and that's when I realized that racism was out there in our little country town. There was a white side and a black side, and my grandfather got ticked off because they wouldn't let my cousins play on the city tennis court. So my grandfather built his own tennis court. He said, 'My kids can have anything other kids can have!' We played tennis every weekend. You've got to work at it to be good."

—BILL HOLLOMAN

HOW TO HIT A TENNIS SERVE

Step 1: Set your feet. Stand with your kicks shoulder-width apart just behind the baseline on either side of the center mark. (Scoot to the right if you're serving into the left box, or to the left if you're serving into the right one.) Your dominant rear foot should be parallel to the baseline, and your weaker front foot should be turned at about a forty-five-degree angle.

Step 2: Grip your racket. Wrap your dominant hand around your racket so the face of the racket is perpendicular to the floor. If your racket had blades around its edges, you'd be able to chop wood with it.

Step 3: Choose your target. Without being too obvious and telegraphing your serve to your opponent, focus on where you'd like your serve to land. Once you choose your spot, don't waver.

Step 4: Toss your ball. Hold the tennis ball in your weaker hand against the strings of your racket. Then throw it high up into the air one to two feet in front of you, keeping your eye on it the entire time.

Step 5: Whack it. As your ball rises into the air, bend your knees. When it reaches its peak, spring upward and forward, extend your arm to strike the ball at the highest point possible, and follow through.

More Handy Tips

- To practice your serve, break it down. Master your toss; then master your swing.

- Since you've got two shots to ace your serve, go big on the first one. If you default, you've got another try.

- Stay on your toes. Flat-footed tennis players get beat every time.

- Keep your grip on your racket loose, until you lift it to strike the ball. That'll help keep everything else, and particularly your shoulders, loose too.

- Never curse on the court. Don't ever #%^&*! do it.

Play Fair

· · ·

"Play hard, accomplish your goals, and yet be humble in the eyes of your opponents."
—Bob Kelly

How to Be a Good Sport

Step 1: Play fairly. Cheating only proves one thing: You're not strong enough, fast enough, or smart enough to win the game on your own. A win by dubious means is not a win at all, and even if no one else knows what you did to break the rules, you will, and it won't feel good. Know the rules, and abide by them, and you'll be able to relish every victory, knowing you played your best.

Step 2: Respect your opponent. You may feel like you want to mop the floor with him or humiliate him in front of a crowd, but remember that without a competitor, you wouldn't have a game to play at all. Be thankful for the other team, and respect their efforts and abilities. Then you can beat them.

Step 3: Be gracious in your losses. If the game didn't go your way, there's nothing you can do but accept it. No tears, no temper tantrums, no fighting. Simply hold your head up high, thank your opponent for a good match, and vow to play harder next time.

Step 4: Be humble in your victories. If the game did go your way, good for you! Now hold your head up high, thank your opponent for a good match, and vow to play harder next time. You can break out your happy dance later, after the other team has gone home.

More Handy Tips

- Listen to your coaches and the officials. Backtalk during a match is bad form, even if you think you know better. If you're tempted to trash-talk, pretend your grandmother is on the sidelines listening to your every word. If your grandmother swears like a sailor, then imagine the string of curses she'll let out if she catches you misbehaving during the game.

- Share the glory. If you're playing a team sport, remember that it takes an entire team, not just one person, to win the game.

- Have fun! After all, that's the whole point, isn't it?

Cheer On

• • •

"To be a good fan, you've got to know the game. Know the game!"
—Angel Rodriguez

How to Be a Good Fan

Step 1: Stay positive. Your team needs you, so cheer them on when something goes well and cheer them up when something goes wrong. Heckling from the stands, against the players (on your team or the opposing team), coaches, fans, or, yes, even referees, only poisons the atmosphere and makes the day miserable for everyone, including you. Keep your words positive, and a good day will be had by all.

Step 2: Be loyal. You're not a good fan if you're only in the stands when the team is on top. Underdogs need some love, too, and watching players grow year after year is one of the greatest pleasures in spectator sports. Along those lines, unless it's absolutely necessary, never leave a game early, no matter what the score.

Step 3: Mind your manners. Just because you're at a sporting event doesn't mean all social graces fall by the wayside. If you find yourself screaming until you're red in the face, you're probably yelling too much. Be considerate of those around you, which also means keeping your mouth clean, both physically and verbally. Nobody wants you spitting nachos all over them, and nobody wants to hear you curse a blue streak, especially if there are kids around.

More Handy Tips

- Stay sober. Go ahead and enjoy a few ice-cold ones. Just don't overdo it, or you may get yourself into trouble.

- Wear your team colors on your back (in the form of a shirt, not body paint, unless, of course, you're superfit, in college, it's warm out, and you don't have a date later).

- Stay in your seat, so the fans behind you can see the game as well as you can. And never run onto the field or court.

- Know when to keep your mouth shut. If you're at your kid's game, leave the coaching to the coaches and the refereeing to the refs. Your *only* job is to support and encourage your child.

Make a Splash

· · ·

"I was an excellent swimmer, and we had a diving platform out in the bay. We did backflips, double flips, full gainers. We didn't even know there was such a thing as proper form. You'd do it and that was it. Just don't do a belly flopper."
—Buck Buchanan

How to Do a Backflip

Step 1: Get a crowd. It's fun doing backflips on your own, but it's even more fun when you've got a bunch of people watching you, especially if some of those people are good-looking.

Step 2: Walk the plank. Suck in your gut and march yourself out to the end of the diving board. When you get there, turn around so your bum is facing the water. Extend both arms in front of you for balance, and scoot yourself to the very edge, so only the balls of your feet are on the board while your heels are hanging off.

Step 3: Say a little prayer. Something along the lines of "Please do not let me wipe out in front of all these people" usually works well.

Step 4: Jump. Gently bounce on the board, feeling light, happy, and hopeful. When you're ready to go, rise up onto your toes, then bend your knees, bringing your arms to your sides or slightly behind you. Now, in one fluid motion, spring upward and backward, throwing your arms overhead.

Step 5: Tuck. At the peak of your jump, tuck your knees to your chest, wrapping your arms around them for style points.

Step 6: Enter the water. Once your body has made one full rotation, extend your legs toward the water, bring your arms to your sides, and lean forward slightly. All of those moves will help you slow your rotation, so you don't overspin and end up with a bright red back. The smaller the splash, the better your flip.

Step 7: Come up smiling.

More Handy Tips

- As long as you jump up *and* back, you won't hit your head on the board. Confidence is your friend when it comes to doing a backflip.

- Make sure the water you're jumping into is deep enough. Duh.

- If you under-rotate and belly flop, you may be tempted to stay underwater for a few extra seconds before surfacing in hopes that your crowd will forget about your failed flip. Fat chance. You know that sucker's going on YouTube. You might as well embrace it, so come up big and show off your red tummy.

Control Your Balls

· · ·

"Don't knock anybody. They might be bad one day but good the next."
—AL SULKA

HOW TO PLAY BOCCE

Step 1: Find a court. Or make one. All you need is a long flat stretch of grass, sand, dirt, or pavement, and a set of balls. Regulation courts are about eighty-seven feet long by thirteen feet wide and edged with wooden boards, but you can use whatever space you've got. Draw a line to mark half-court, if there's not one already.

Step 2: Choose teams. You'll need two teams with one, two, or four players on each. Bocce is a game of finesse and strategy, so don't overlook the wimpy-looking guys or gals. They may be ringers for all you know. Divide the balls by color, accordingly, four to each side.

Step 3: Throw the pallino, which is the little ball. To decide who gets to do it, flip a coin. The winner gets the toss and the pallino must pass the half-court line and rest twelve inches or more from the edge of the court. If it doesn't, the pallino goes to the opposing team, which may try again.

Step 4: Throw the first bocce ball. Any member of the team who originally tossed the pallino, successfully or not, gets the first shot at it. The goal: Get your bocce ball as close as possible to the pallino. Since no other balls have been thrown yet, the first ball is considered "inside," because it is the closest ball to the pallino. Who cares if it's by default! Yay, you! At the end of the game, your team will get a point for every inside ball, or every ball you've landed closer to the pallino than your opponent.

Step 5: Hold your breath and allow the other team to throw. They're going to try to do one of three things: (1) Land their bocce ball closer to the pallino than yours; (2) use their ball to knock yours away; (3) use their ball to knock the pallino away from yours. If they're successful at any of these, and their ball is closer to the pallino than yours, then play reverts to you. If your ball is still inside, the opposing team continues to throw until they've used all their balls. Bottom line: Whichever team is outside continues to throw until they either run out of balls or land inside.

Step 6: Rack up points. If the inside team has any balls left after the outside team has thrown all of theirs, they must play their balls now. You'll get a point for each ball you land inside, but don't get too cocky or you may knock away the pallino or your team's closest ball and lose the game.

Step 7: Score the match. After all eight bocce balls have been played, a representative from each team must assess the court. Each team gets one point for every bocce ball it has landed closer to the pallino than their opponents, with a maximum score of four points per round.

Step 8: Play again, switching sides of the court. The first team to win twelve or fifteen points, your choice, wins the game.

More Handy Tips

- *Bocce* rhymes with *splotchy*, not *gross*.

- Though all balls must be lobbed or rolled underhand, you may grip them underneath or overtop (to create a backspin).

- Whenever a bocce ball hits the backboard without first hitting any other balls, it's considered dead and removed from play. The same team should throw again.

- For more information on bocce, visit the United States Bocce Federation at www.bocce.com.

- Bocce is best played while sipping a Bocce Ball cocktail: Pour 1½ ounces of vodka, ½ ounce of amaretto, and fresh orange juice over ice; shake. Add a splash of club soda and garnish with an orange slice.

8

Dressing

. . .

*When you look in the mirror and feel proud,
you'll have the confidence to take on the world.*

Be Dapper

...

"It's sometimes tough to find self-confidence. As far as dressing correctly in public, you've got to feel good about yourself. If you feel like you look well, you can fit into the crowds and become an extrovert. If you feel like you look bad, it's tough to assimilate."

—BOB KELLY

HOW TO TIE FOUR TIE KNOTS

The Windsor

The biggest, most powerful knot (perfect for job interviews or Senate confirmation hearings), it works well on a shirt with a wide collar.

Step 1: Pop your collar. Standing in front of a mirror, give yourself a wink, be sure nobody just saw you do that, then turn up your collar and drape the tie around your neck with the fat end on your right and the skinny end on your left. Tug the fat end down so it's a good eighteen inches or so below the skinny end.

Step 2: Cross the fat end over the skinny end. Then bring it up through the neck loop and drop it down the front. So far, so good.

Step 3: Swing the fat end to the left, then pass it under the skinny end to the right. Now bring the fat end in front and drop it down through your neck loop. You'll know you've done it right if the skinny end of your tie is now on top and the fat end is underneath and facing the wrong way.

Step 4: Swing the fat end to the left once more, pass it over the skinny end to the right, and bring it up through the neck loop, tucking the fat end through the resulting triangle-shaped knot. Tighten, and scoot it up to your neck.

Step 5: Turn your collar down and test your swagger. You'll need it with that knot.

The Half-Windsor

As the Windsor's little brother, this knot gets along with every shirt, especially lighter ones, and goes with every occasion.

Step 1: Pop your collar, and drape the tie around your neck with the fat end on your right and the skinny end on your left. Tug the fat end down so it's a good twelve to fifteen inches below the skinny end.

Step 2: Swing the fat end over the skinny end to the left and pass it up through the neck loop, allowing the fat end to drop down in the front.

Step 3: Swing the fat end to the left, then pass it under the skinny end to the right, back over the skinny end to the left, and up through the neck loop.

Step 4: Tuck the fat end of your tie through the resulting knot. Tighten it, scoot it up, unpop your collar, point to yourself in the mirror, and make that cheek-sucking sound that horse trainers make when they want their horses to run. You look like a stallion.

The Four-in-Hand

The Four-in-Hand is the skinny jeans of tie knots: It's superhip, but you've got to have the right look to pull it off.

Step 1: Pop your collar and drape the tie around your neck so the fat end hangs on your right, about ten inches below the skinny end.

Step 2: Cross the fat end over the skinny end to the left, back under the skinny end to the right, and back over the skinny end to the left.

Step 3: Pass the fat end up through the neck loop, and carefully tuck it through the resulting knot in the front. Put on your silver kicks and live it up.

The Bow Tie

The perfect knot for a black-tie event, a White House dinner, or a hipster potluck.

Step 1: Drape the bow tie around your neck with one end hanging about 1½ inches below the other.

Step 2: Cross the long end over the short end, bring it up through the neck loop, and pull both ends so it's tight against your neck.

Step 3: Grasp the short end of the tie (now the end lying against your shirt), then fold it like an accordion so the bow of the tie is pressed against the center of your neck. Hold it there with the thumb and forefinger of your right hand.

Step 4: Drape the top end of your tie over your newly formed bow. Then squeeze both ends of your bow together, like butterfly wings, leaving the top end draped between them.

Step 5: Pull your butterfly wings gently away from your neck, and you'll see a hole open up behind them. Tuck the top (not the bottom) of the dangling end of the bow tie through that hole.

Step 6: Cinch and straighten. You've got to be really elegant or supersmart to pull off this tie. Bonus points if you're both.

More Handy Tips

- Always fasten the top button of your collar before tightening your tie.

- A good knot creates a dimple in the center of your tie. Look for one.

- Even though you may be tempted to leave your tie knotted after you take it off, don't do it. You'll look like a wrinkled mess next time you put it on, and, really, how hard was it to tie? Instead, roll up your tie, starting at the skinny end, and lay it seam-side down in a drawer until your next fancy occasion.

Mind the Details

• • •

"The little things matter: the handkerchief in the pocket, the tie, the cuff links. Cuff links give you style. Most of my shirts have them."
—BILL HOLLOMAN

HOW TO WEAR CUFF LINKS

Step 1: Choose your shirt. If you want to bring your best to a formal party or just add a dash of dapper to an everyday outfit, a flashy pair of cuff links will do you fine. Since they take the place of buttons, you'll need a special shirt: one with French cuffs, or giant cuffs with holes at the wrist instead of buttons.

Step 2: Line up your holes. Put on your shirt and fold the cuffs in half. Make sure all four holes, two on each side, are in line and ready to receive the cuff link.

Step 3: Insert your cuff link. If you're using a swivel cuff link, turn the lever in line with the studs so that the link is straight, and stick it through all four holes. Once the stud emerges from the other side, pull the swivel out so it forms a T to secure your shirt. Repeat on the other arm.

Step 4: Look in the mirror. Helllooo handsome!

More Handy Tips

- Cuff links should give a little flash, but shouldn't steal the show. Match 'em up with your shirt or tie.

- You can buy expensive cuff links at high-end stores and fancy haberdasheries, but if you want to go retro you can often find good ones in your local thrift shop or flea market.

- The swivel post is the most common style of cuff link. Once you get the hang of them, you may want to experiment with button style (two "buttons" linked with a chain), clip cuff links (ornamental front and back that clip together inside), and knot cuff links (silk cord held together with knots).

Top It Off

. . .

"With every suit, I'd wear a different hat. I'd go to the mirror and look at myself. It's got to tilt at just the right angle."
—ANGEL RODRIGUEZ

HOW TO WEAR A HAT

Step 1: Check the mirror. To buy a lid that flatters your dome, you've got to take into account what you've got going on up there. Stare at your face in the mirror and say "Bloody Mary" three times. Just kidding. Don't do that or a ghost might show up. Instead, look at the shape of your face. If you've got a long one, wear a hat with a big brim. If you've got a round mug, go for a short hat with a smaller brim. If you've got a square face, offset your angles with a big ol' round topper.

Step 2: Know the styles. Your hat says something about not only your sense of fashion, but also the way you perceive yourself. Match it to your outfit—and your personality.

The Fedora: This sophisticated hat can be worn year-round (straw in summer, felt in winter). Hotties—think Frank Sinatra, Humphrey Bogart, Don Draper—prefer it tipped a bit to the side. Best for formal occasions. Or breaking hearts.

The Porkpie: Buster Keaton, jazz great Lester Young, British punks—many rule breakers have donned the porkpie. Maybe it's because the short-crowned hat with the short round brim makes you look more innocent than others might suspect.

The Panama: Perfect for summer, this straw hat is classic, it's lightweight, and it protects your head from the heat and sun. Pair it with a suit and you're ready to make history, just like Teddy Roosevelt.

The Newsboy Cap: Channel Gatsby and don this casual cap in cooler weather with a suit or sweater, or out on the golf course. Cock it to the side if you're feeling jaunty.

The Hunting Cap: Elmer Fudd may not be a style icon, but at least his ear flaps are keeping him toasty. A leather-and-fur number (pleather-and-faux-fur, if you prefer) works with suits, and plaids can be rocked when you're off the clock.

Step 3: Tilt it just so. If you're all business, wear your hat with the brim evenly pointing forward in the middle of your forehead. If you're a freewheelin' kinda guy, or you're pairing your hat with jeans and a T-shirt, tilt it back a bit to flash those baby blues (or greens or browns or hazels). If you're feeling mysterious, or you're in hiding from the feds, pull your cap down a bit lower on your forehead and tip it to the side.

Step 4: Mind your manners. If you're a man, always remove your cap whenever you enter a restaurant, a church, or any room of any building. Of course, keep it off while you eat, work, pray, or sing (or mouth the words to) the national anthem. And tip or raise it when passing a beautiful woman on the street. If you're a woman, lucky you. You don't have to remove your hat at any time (not even in church), which doesn't seem quite fair to the lads. Of course, men don't have to shave their legs, either, so you win some, you lose some. You win at hats.

More Handy Tips

- A professional hatter—the guy who actually makes them by stretching the felt over a wooden block, not the guy who sets them on top of Styrofoam heads in the mall—will help you find the perfect hat for your face and style. Trust him, and pony up. A good hat will last you forever.

- If you can't find a fancy hat store, make your way to the nearest thrift shop for a retro find. Just bring an outspoken but kind friend who can steer you in the right direction.

- Try different styles. Don't wear a newsboy cap or a cowboy hat every single day of your life to every event in your life. Branch out.

Look Sharp

• • •

"Dress well. Dress the best you can! It means that you represent something."
—Angel Rodriguez

How to Dress for a Date

Step 1: Check your inventory. Stand in front of your closet and take a good honest look at what you've got to work with. Then take everything you've already worn and put it in the hamper and don't even consider reaching for anything made of sweat-suit material. Hopefully, once you eliminate the dirties and the sweats, you've got a few tops, bottoms, and jackets left.

Step 2: Step it up. You want your date to know that you put in extra effort to look your best. So don't wear what you always wear every single day or what you've already been wearing all day long. To look fine (and, let's be frank, kissable), you've got to take your style, whatever that happens to be, up a notch. If you're a prep, put on trousers, a button-down shirt, and maybe even a jacket. If you're a jock, wear your best jeans and try a shirt with a collar. If you're a goth, put on a fresh coat of black nail polish and slip a rose into your trench-coat pocket. Hey, whatever works.

Step 3: Put your best foot forward. Do not show up for a date in ratty, old, smelly, grass-stained sneakers. Make sure your kicks are fresh and, if necessary, polished.

Step 4: Practice the ol' "How you doin'?" in the bathroom mirror a few times, to get your confidence up, before you go. That's right, "How you doin'?" Uh-huh.

More Handy Tips

- Never wear flip-flops or sandals on a date, unless you're going to the beach and you've recently cut your toenails. Even then, it's iffy.

- Always shower and shave before a date, and put on clean undies even if you think the ones you already have on are okay.

- A dab of cologne is nice, but don't overdo it, Romeo. See page 120 for advice on how to put on just the right amount.

- Be yourself, and look like your best you. Never dress like someone else, unless of course you're going to a costume party.

Clean Up

. . .

"Don't push your clothes down tight in the washer. Don't overload the dryer, either. When you're done, your clothes will smell better than this shirt I've got on."
—Philip Spooner

How to Do Laundry

Step 1: Memorize this page. Laundry may be boring business, but you've got to learn how to do it, unless you want to live with your mom forever, pay expensive weekly laundry bills, or wear gray holey undies for the rest of your life. Scared? Good. Read on.

Step 2: Sort it out. Pull everything out of your hamper and divide your dirties into three piles on the floor: whites, dark colors, and reds. You'll wash each load separately to keep your colors bright and your whites white. As you're sorting, check the pockets to make sure they're empty—and check the tags, too, looking for any clothes that say DRY CLEAN ONLY. Set those fancy duds aside.

Step 3: Fill the washer. Toss, don't pack, your dirty clothes into the washing machine. If you try to stuff too much stuff in there, the soap and water won't have room to circulate and all of your clothes will be as filthy at the end of the cycle as they were at the beginning. Also, you might break your washer. If everything doesn't fit in one load, do a second. No big wup.

Step 4: Add soap. Most home washers (and every public washer at the Laundromat or in your dorm or apartment building) can handle regular laundry soap, but some washers require high-efficiency soap. If you're not sure which kind yours takes, check the manual. Then add some bubbly. If your washer has a specially marked spot for soap, well, pour it in there then. If not, pour it directly onto your dirty clothes. How much soap depends on which kind you're using. Just read the back of the bottle for the precise measurement.

Step 5: Set the temp. Wash whites in hot water, and colors in warm or cold.

Step 6: Wait. Go do something else for an hour, like have a cocktail (page 246) or clean your house (page 41) (or both), while your clothes clean themselves. See? This isn't too hard now, is it?

Step 7: Dry your clothes. When the wash cycle finishes, transfer your damp clothes to the dryer, being sure to separate any clothes that are labeled LAY FLAT TO DRY or LINE DRY. Also, set aside any items that already fit a little too snugly, as drying could cause them to shrink. Hang those up accordingly. Once you've put all of your dryables in the dryer, add a sheet of fabric softener, and start the cycle on MEDIUM to avoid overdrying or wrinkles.

Step 8: Put it away. After your clothes are dry, take them out of the dryer immediately and hang them up or fold and put them away. (If you leave them in the dryer overnight, they'll wrinkle and you'll either have to iron everything or start all over again.)

More Handy Tips

- If your clothes, no matter the color, are only slightly dirty, you can shave a few bucks off your gas or electric bill and wash them in cold water.

- To make your whites whiter, add bleach to your wash, following the instructions on the bleach and your machine.

- If you want your threads to be extra-soft, add liquid fabric softener, again following the instructions.

- If you want to skip a step, get the detergent with fabric softener or bleach included; just be sure to always use color-safe detergents or all your colors will fade.

- If you have a clothesline (or two trees and a rope), hang your clothes outside to dry. You'll save on electricity costs, and your clothes will smell like pure sunshine.

Go to Press

• • •

*"A guy looks sharper if he's in ironed clothes. When I was in the CCC
[Civilian Conservation Corps], I had a side job. I used to iron shirts for
fifteen cents and pants for ten cents. I'd have to put three pleats in the back
and one on each pocket. We had no electricity, so you had to heat the irons on
a stove. Later, I used to iron my daughter's pleated skirts for school. One day,
the nun said to her, 'Boy, your mother does a good job!' She said, 'My dad
does it!' I was so proud."*

—AL SULKA

HOW TO IRON A SHIRT

Step 1: Set up your ironing board in a clean, uncluttered spot next to
an outlet. Fill your iron with water and plug it in. Crank it to the appropriate temperature, as recommended on the label of your shirt. If
your iron is too hot, you'll torch your shirt. Too cold, and you'll lose
the war on wrinkles.

Step 2: Pop the collar as if it were 1983. Lay your unbuttoned shirt,
faceup, on the board and spread the collar flat. Using small circular motions, iron the collar from the center toward each point. Flip it and repeat.

Step 3: Do the yoke. Pull the shoulder of your shirt over the pointy
end of the board, and iron the piece of material that connects the collar to the body. Switch shoulders and repeat.

Step 4: Smooth the sleeves. Grab the right one and, aligning the
seam along the underarm, from pit to cuff, spread it flat on the board.

Work your iron in tiny circles from the shoulder to (but not over) the cuff.

Step 5: Cock the cuffs. Spread them flat and iron from the sleeve's seam to the edge. Flip it and repeat. If you have folded cuffs, fold now and iron just the crease.

Step 6: Iron the front and back. If you're right-handed, drape the right panel of your shirt's front over the board, collar toward the pointy end, allowing the rest of the shirt to hang in front of you. (If you're a lefty, start with the left front panel.) Work your iron in small circular motions from the top to the tail. Rotate the shirt over the board to iron the back. Rotate again to iron the front left panel.

Step 7: Wear immediately or hang on a hanger, preferably a wooden one.

More Handy Tips

- If you don't have an ironing board, a hard flat surface, covered with a clean dry towel, will do in a pinch.

- Iron only clean shirts. If you try to press a dirty one, you'll just set in the stains forever.

- Spritz stubborn wrinkles with a water bottle before ironing.

- To iron around buttons, poke the point of your iron, held flat, between each, angling up and down with every pass. Don't plow over them or they could break.

Thread the Needle

· · ·

"You don't really get a handle on most tasks until it looks like you're doing them very easily. That's one of the tricks of acquiring new skills: Do it, fix it, and then be confident that you can do it better again the next time when you need to."

—FRANK WALTER

HOW TO SEW A BUTTON

Step 1: Gather your supplies. You'll need a replacement button, a needle, about two feet of matching thread, and a pair of scissors.

Step 2: Thread the needle, pulling one end of the thread through to meet the other. Knot the ends together by making a loop and pulling the tails through. Knot once more, and trim off any excess.

Step 3: Locate your button's proper spot by eyeballing where it was before it fell off. Look for either some old broken thread (and remove it) or a few tiny holes in the fabric from where the thread once was. If you can't see where it should go, fasten your other buttons, pass a pin through the hole of the renegade, and mark that spot with chalk or pencil.

Step 4: Push your needle up through the back of the fabric to the front, pulling the thread all the way through. Slide your button on down the thread to meet the fabric.

Step 5: Once you've got your button in place and the holes lined up, push your needle down through the opposite hole (either diagonally or adjacently to match your other buttons) and out the back of the fabric. Repeat four times, pulling the thread tight enough so that your button doesn't dangle but loose enough so that your fabric doesn't pucker. If you have a four-hole button, switch hole-pairs and repeat.

Step 6: For the finishing touch, push your needle up through the back of the fabric to the front but *not* through any buttonholes. Just let it dangle out the side. Pull your button away from the fabric and wrap your thread tightly around the shank (aka the thread between the button and fabric) six times.

Step 7: Press your needle through the shank twice. Snip the thread—no need to knot.

Step 8: Get dressed, feel proud, look like a million bucks.

More Handy Tips

• If you can't find your missing button, check inside your shirt for replacement buttons. Manufacturers, at least the nice ones, will stash a few extras inside, usually along the side or bottom seam.

• If you lose a noticeable button, can't find a replacement, and are just hanging in the wind, snip one from a less-conspicuous spot, like the very bottom of your shirt or a cuff—preferably one you'll later roll up. That'll buy you a little time to replace the button.

• If you're sewing a button onto a thicker fabric, place a matchstick or toothpick on the button and sew over it to help you maintain the proper spacing. Then remove the spacer before winding the thread around the shank.

Put Your Best Foot Forward

. . .

"A lot of people did the spit shine in the marine corps because they didn't have anything else to do. There was no TV, no books, no nothing, so the entertainment was to get a polish rag and spit-shine your shoes."
—Chuck Tatum

How to Shine Shoes

Step 1: Wipe down your kicks, especially the heel and sole, with a soft cotton cloth to remove all dust and dirt.

Step 2: Wrap a soft cotton rag or old sock (ahem, a clean one) around your index and middle fingers.

Step 3: Dip your rag into a cup of room-temperature water, dab it into your shoe polish, and dip it back into the water. It should be damp, not soaking.

Step 4: Placing your opposite hand into the shoe for stability, start applying polish, tip-to-heel, using a tiny circular motion. Make several passes over the same small area before moving to the next.

Step 5: After polishing the entire shoe, dampen a clean cloth and make one even pass over the shoe to prevent drops or streaks.

Step 6: Allow the shoes to dry for ten minutes.

Step 7: Buff both sides of each shoe with a horsehair polishing brush or a buffing cloth.

Step 8: To enhance the shine, from a seated position, place the shoe between your knees. Holding panty hose or a buffing cloth with both hands, slide it back and forth over the toe. To be supercool, snap the cloth.

More Handy Tips

- If you get rock salt on leather shoes, add a tablespoon of vinegar to a cup of water; soak a cotton ball or paper towel in this, then use it to gently wipe the salt away. Allow the leather to dry before polishing.

- Buff scuffs with a dab of toothpaste and a moist rag. Wipe clean.

9

Loving

. . .

This is what life is all about. Get good at it.

Channel Romeo

· · ·

"I used to write love letters, but I had to get in the mood, you know? So I'd look in my big, thick quotation book and I'd find a special quote I liked. I'd put that into the letter and play around with it. As long as I can remember, I called her Mush. And I signed my letters, 'Lovez ya, your JoJo.'"
—Joe Toth

How to Write a Love Letter

Step 1: Put pen to paper. After all, it's a love *letter*, not a love email or, for goodness' sake, a love text, if such a thing exists (and for the record, it shouldn't). Instead of reaching for your phone or laptop, reach for a nice, heavyweight unlined piece of paper and a black pen. Classic.

Step 2: Address the letter. "Dear So-and-So" will be fine, but if you have a pet name for your beloved, now's the time to use it.

Step 3: Let your feelings flow. You know all those things you wanted to say in person but were too shy or scared to say? Now's the time to let them out. Pour your heart out onto the paper without being too worried about how it reads. Let's say you're writing to a woman. Tell her why you're writing her this letter, how she makes you feel, how you feel when you're not with her, what qualities you love in her. (No, her boobs are not one of the qualities you should mention here.) Include those little things she does that make your heart race, like the way she laughs or smiles.

Step 4: Close your letter. Sign it in a way that leaves your sweetie swooning. "With love" is fine, but "forever yours" is better.

Step 5: Drop it in the mail, hold your breath, and wait for a response.

More Handy Tips

- Try to spell as best you can, but don't be paralyzed by your words or your grammar. If the object of your affection is going to judge you on those things, and not on the emotion behind your words, you're writing to the wrong person anyway.

- Don't confuse love with lust. If your love letter reads like some sort of erotic wish list, go take a cold shower and try it again later.

- Don't just send love letters when your beloved is far away. Leave one on your honey's bedside table, slip one in her lunch bag, or drop one in the mail, even if you live together, whenever you feel inspired. It only takes a few minutes, and the payoff will be well worth it. A love letter will be more cherished than any other gift you could ever give, because opening up your heart to someone else takes courage and trust, and both are far more valuable than money.

Go Courting

· · ·

"I met my wife at a neighborhood carnival. We got talking and then the next thing you know, we were sort of dating. I liked her right away. I used to walk two miles to go see her! I didn't have no money, so I'd go over to her house and sit on her front porch. You couldn't sit close, either! Her mother would look out the window."

—AL SULKA

HOW TO PLAN A DATE

Step 1: Be considerate. When deciding what to do, keep your date's interests in mind. Don't get baseball tickets for a ballet fan or plan a day of window-shopping for a nature lover. If you're not sure what she likes yet, plan something neutral, like a dinner at an Italian restaurant or a picnic in the park. That way, you'll have a chance to talk and learn more about each other.

Step 2: Get creative. No one is going to dock you points for showing up with roses and having reservations at a fancy restaurant, but you might score bigger if you do something original: take a romantic boat ride, build a bonfire on the beach, cook a meal together. Not only will it make the date more memorable, but you're also signaling that you're one of a kind.

Step 3: Dress up. Now that you've gotten some kind soul to agree to spend a few hours with you, prove to her that she made the right decision by cleaning up and dressing up. Looking sharp lets your date know you care.

Step 4: Pick her up. Show up at her front door on time. No honking from your car or texting from the street.

Step 5: Use good manners. Open doors. Walk beside her, and offer her your arm. Listen more than you talk. And keep the drinking to a minimum. Showing your respect, more than anything else, will ensure that you get another date soon.

Step 6: Host with the most. Since you requested the date, be prepared to foot the bill for the evening. If she offers to chip in, tell her it'd be your privilege and pleasure to pay. It's good manners, and it shows you're invested. Maybe she'll treat you next time.

Step 7: Walk her to her door, thank her for the date, and—if all went well and the moment is right—go in for a quick kiss. You'll know the moment is wrong if it seems like she can't get in the door fast enough, she reaches out to shake your hand, or she's holding her hand in front of her face, waving good-bye to you. You'll know it's right if she lingers a little too long or turns her mouth toward yours or you've both said good-bye and are still standing there staring at each other, smiling.

Step 8: Follow up. Call her the next day, or the day after that, and if she answers, ask her out again.

More Handy Tips

- If you need to change the *she*s to *he*s, well, la-di-da. The same rules still apply.

- Make your date as interactive as possible. Going to a movie or concert can be fun, but it's very difficult to get to know someone without talking for two hours. If you do plan a movie or concert date, at least have dessert afterward.

- A fancy date doesn't guarantee a good date. You'll be judged more by how much thought you put into planning it and how well you behaved when you were together than by the price tag of the evening. Fancy gifts are nice, if you can swing them, but if your honey is more impressed with your wallet than your will, search for another sweetheart.

Win Hearts

• • •

"I bought her mother a dozen roses. Boy, I made a lot of points with her."
—JOE TOTH

HOW TO BUY FLOWERS

Step 1: Plan ahead. If you want to bring a special someone flowers, don't just pluck them from a neighbor's yard or, worse, the flowerpot on the front porch. Instead, before you show up at the front door, stop by your local flower shop (or even just a corner store). When you arrive with flowers wrapped in pretty paper, it shows that you're thoughtful and trying to make a good impression.

Step 2: Choose a bouquet. If you're not sure which kind of flowers to buy, go with what you like; if they all look pretty much the same to you, ask the shopkeeper for guidance. As a general rule, though, stay away from carnations and baby's breath, unless you're trying to stir up flashbacks from senior prom. Red roses are very meaningful, so if you're just trying to brighten someone's day and not promise your everlasting love, choose any colorful bunch: daisies, wildflowers, hydrangeas.

Step 3: Speak in secret code, if you'd like. During Victorian times, every flower carried a certain message. If you want to add another layer of meaning to your gift, here are a few flowers and their significances:

Calla lilies: "You are just so beautiful."

Daisies: "I love your sweet innocence."

Daffodils: "This is the start of something good."

Lavender: "Wishing you the best of luck!"

Lilacs: "I think I'm falling in love with you—and I've never felt this way before."

Peonies: "Here's to your good health and happiness."

Red roses: "I like you. Like, really really *really* like you."

Pink roses: "You are just so graceful."

White roses: "When I say, 'I love you,' you can trust I mean it."

Yellow roses: "Thanks for being my friend."

Red tulips: "I'll love you forever."

Violets: "I'll always be there for you."

Step 4: Make it a habit. Flowers shouldn't just be hallmarks of a first date. They're even more delightful if they're unexpected. A bunch won't cost you much more than ten or twenty bucks, and the smile on your sweetie's face will be worth every penny.

More Handy Tips

- Flowers work after a date, too. Nothing says "I had a nice time" better than a sweet bouquet the day after with a nice note.

- Don't have flowers delivered after a fight in hopes that they will make everything better. They might help, depending on your honey, but they're not magic. If you've done something wrong, it's up to you to make it right.

- If your honey has a green thumb, take her a plant instead. You'll be able to watch it grow as your relationship grows, and no bunches will go to waste.

Be a Gentleman

• • •

"Chivalry is important. You want to make an impression on another person. Demonstrate your respect."
—BUCK BUCHANAN

HOW TO BE CHIVALROUS

Step 1: Have good manners. This means doing the most basic things to make your honey comfortable. Open doors, let her exit the elevator first, lend a hand over a puddle, pull out her chair, help her with her coat, and offer to carry any heavy bags.

Step 2: Stand by her side. Never walk in front of your companion, expecting her to catch up when she can. Instead, offer her your arm and walk alongside her. In tight spots, tip your head, gesture with your hand, and say, "After you." She'll go crazy for it. (And you get to walk behind her, too, which is awesome if she's your date.)

Step 3: Put her needs first. Don't worry about how much fun you're having at every moment. Instead, make sure she feels comfortable and happy, and you'll both be sure to have a good time.

Step 4: Keep your word. If you say you'll be somewhere at seven o'clock, be there at seven. If you are going to be late, call. Your word is your honor. Protect its worth.

More Handy Tips

- Chivalry extends from your personal relationships to your professional ones. It's not so much about opening doors for women as about the way you are in the world. Strive to treat all others with respect, be loyal and trustworthy, and have the courage to express yourself in every part of your life.

- If your beloved is strong and independent-minded, that's awesome—but it's not your free ticket to lazy land. She still wants to be treated with respect, consideration, and affection. If you're lucky, she'll treat you the same way, too.

Find the One

· · ·

"My friend and I were talking about who would be your favorite wife? I said I'd marry Sandy Nussel and worry about falling in love with her later. She was so beautiful, and I admired her all through high school. A week later, I got a postcard from her. We went to dinner and then to the ball game. Two dates later, I proposed, and she said yes! That was in June or July and we got married that November. It was a quick courtship, but when you know you know. And how! I picked her up and we went to have a bite to eat. We just sat there looking at each other and we couldn't even find words. We couldn't even breathe. I feel it now even."

—Bob Kelly

How to Know When to Take the Plunge

Step 1: Find a nice one. Attraction certainly helps, but if you're looking for a runway model with an MBA who moonlights as both a chef and stand-up comic, then you might be looking an awfully long time. Remember, you're marrying a real person, not a lead in a romantic comedy. Find someone who is kind, caring, loyal, and, above all, makes you feel like a better version of yourself.

Step 2: Fall in love. This part happens naturally, but it's up to you to recognize it when it does. Unlike lust, which is wonderful but short-lived, love lasts and is undeterred by bad haircuts, bad habits, failed diets, lost jobs, or difficult in-laws. In fact, love makes all the good times that much better and all the bad times less painful. Can you imagine your life without this person? If not, congrats: You're in love. If so, it's back to the dating pool with you. When you find someone you not only want, but need, to be with, whom you enjoy and respect, and who makes your world suddenly seem full of possibility, that's love. When you feel it, you'll know you want to hang on to it.

Step 3: Wait for the right moment. There's no rush. Starting a life with someone else is easier if you have a good education, a decent job, and a place to live, but only you will know when the time is right. Do what feels comfortable for you.

More Handy Tips

- Match up. Similar values, faiths, goals, and interests help a relationship thrive. If you don't share these things, you should at least share a healthy appreciation of each other's core beliefs.

- If you found a nice one, fell in love, and the moment is right, then spring for the ring. She'll have it forever, so make it a beauty. But if she's more concerned with the size of the rock than the size of your heart, go back to step 1.

Make Love Last

. . .

"We kiss every night. Every night before you go to bed, you've got to kiss."
—Joe Toth

HOW TO KINDLE ROMANCE

Step 1: Set aside one night every month (more frequently, if you can swing it) and make it known to your honey that it's "your night." Raise expectations by marking it on your calendar and talking up the evening (preferably while wiggling your eyebrows up and down).

Step 2: Eliminate distractions. Send the kids off to a friend's or relative's house for the night. Turn off the television, shut down your computer, and silence the phones. Showing your honey that he or she is a priority and that there's nowhere else you'd rather be in the world is a big turn-on.

Step 3: Set the mood according to your sweetie's taste. Punk rock and Pabst Blue Ribbon may put many more stars in her eyes than, say, Billie Holiday and bubbly. Don't get saddled by convention. And don't think you have to get too baum-chicka-baum-baum, either. Just find something that suits you both. Or take turns. There's nothing wrong with beer one night and champagne the next.

Step 4: Activate your senses. That may mean enjoying a delicious meal, taking a bath, giving a backrub, or wink, wink, slipping into something a little more comfortable. A short warning: Remember that the sole purpose of the evening is not to simply eat dinner. Take care not to overindulge, in food or drink, lest your stomach steal the spotlight from your sweetie.

Step 5: Surely, dear reader, you can figure this one out on your own. And if you can't, wait a few years and try again. It will come to you.

More Handy Tips

- Trade planning duties. You take charge one night, and allow your honey to plan the next. If she's stumped, tell her what you like. That way, you'll both feel catered to and cared for.

- Be flexible. Expectations can bring pressure, so just be loose. Even if the evening doesn't go exactly as planned, it'll still be time together, which is valuable no matter what happens.

Rockabye Baby

• • •

"My son had his days and nights mixed up, so I used to sing to him to put him to sleep. 'Send me a letter, send it by mail, send it in care of Birmingham jail.'"
—AL SULKA

HOW TO HOLD A NEWBORN

Step 1: Give him support. While leaning over your baby as far as you can, gently slide one hand, fingers spread, under his head and neck and the other hand, fingers spread, under his tush. Since his little neck isn't yet strong enough to support his head, you've got to do it for him.

Step 2: Slowly scoop him up toward your body so his tiny body, head included, rests on your chest, and then straighten yourself up.

Step 3: Cradle him in your arms. Always supporting his head, gently lay him down in your arm, so his head is resting in the crook of your elbow and his bottom is snug in your hand. Use the other hand to give him extra support and cuddles.

More Handy Tips

- Newborns startle very easily. Before picking up a baby, talk to him and gently rub his back or belly for a few seconds.

- Be smooth, never sudden or jerky, with your actions, or you'll have a crying baby on your hands.

- If you're a nervous wreck, just stay calm and know that it's up to you to make the infant feel secure and warm. And don't hand him off at the first whimper, or you'll never learn. The more you become comfortable holding him, the more he'll become comfortable being held by you. Stick with it.

Scoop Poop

. . .

"Get everything ahead of time. Once you start, you can't let up too much."
—Philip Spooner

How to Change a Diaper

Step 1: Gather your supplies. You'll need a new diaper, some wipes, and ointment, if necessary.

Step 2: Lay the baby down on a clean, flat surface, and talk to her. Just because you're doing dirty work doesn't mean it's not a great time to bond. Besides, it's much easier changing the diaper of a calm baby than a crying baby.

Step 3: Unfasten the dirty diaper, and take a peek at what happened inside.

Step 4: Gently lift the baby's bottom by carefully grasping both of her ankles with one hand, remove the wet diaper, and lower her down. If, however, she is a stinko mess, fold the diaper in half, so the clean outside of the front is directly under her tush before lowering her. It'll save you from having to clean your changing table, too.

Step 5: Clean the baby's bottom, using a clean, moist wipe. Wipe girls from front to back to prevent infection. (Wipe boys all over.) Apply any diaper rash cream, if your baby's bottom is red or irritated.

Step 6: Lift the baby once more, same way, and slide the new diaper underneath, making sure the sticky tabs are behind her facing up.

Step 7: Fasten the diaper by folding the front half toward her belly, and affixing the tabs to it. It should be snug, but not tight.

More Handy Tips

- Never leave your baby unattended on a changing table, and always keep one hand on her so she doesn't roll off.

- If the baby still has an umbilical cord, fold the front of the diaper down, so it's not pressing on the cord.

- Keep a toy nearby in case your baby needs a little extra distraction.

- If you're changing a boy, wear swimming goggles or, better yet, keep a clean washcloth handy to avoid accidental spurts. Also, point his wee down before closing the diaper, so he'll stay dry.

Tuck In

• • •

"Respect your children. Don't make fun of them if they're scared. Instead, give them a kiss, and they'll feel happy. Do it with love. If you yell at them, they'll never get over their fears."

—ANGEL RODRIGUEZ

HOW TO BANISH MONSTERS UNDER THE BED

Step 1: Understand his fears. You may not see any green, fire-breathing, horned creatures with huge teeth lurking in your kid's room, but these monsters can feel very real to your frightened tot. Don't disregard or belittle his fear. Just telling him that monsters don't exist isn't enough.

Step 2: Take his viewpoint. It may be helpful to crawl in bed with your tot once and see the darkened room as he does, so you can carefully explain to him what every strange shape and shadow is. You don't want to indulge him, but you might even say something like, "Oh, now I can see how you might think that's something scary, but look, it's only your dresser." He'll feel understood and protected, too.

Step 3: Find the source. Go over the day in your head, and try to figure out what your child saw or heard that might've scared him. It could've been a character in a book, something he saw on TV, or even a story he overheard. If you can pinpoint the root of his fear, you can eliminate it.

Step 4: Change his perceptions. If your tot is obsessed with monsters, read him a book about big, cuddly, friendly monsters, so he has a positive image with which to replace his fear. Or one afternoon, have him imagine and draw what his monster best friend might look like and list all the ways he (and his furry friends) are nice.

More Handy Tips

- Unless you want a regular nighttime visitor, don't invite your child into your bed with you. Calm him down, but let him fall asleep again in his own bed.

- As your child gets older, he may begin to fear real threats: fires, earthquakes, burglars. Reassure him as best you can by telling *and* showing him all the ways he's safe.

10

Cooking

. . .

*Learn to wield a knife and spatula,
and you'll never go hungry.*

Be Butch

• • •

"A good cook improvises and always makes it better. He makes it looks easy and does it in such a way that the aroma is through the room so you're hungry before you even start."
—Frank Walter

How to Buy Meat

Step 1: Know where it came from. If you can, steer clear of animals who've spent their entire lives in crowded and confined industrial feed-lots. They've likely been fed the cheapest food possible, which often means they've also been pumped full of hormones, antibiotics, and other drugs to counteract their lousy diet. What's bad for them is bad for you. Instead opt for pasture-raised animals, which are better tasting, healthier, and less harmful to the environment.

Step 2: Choose the grade. After the United States Department of Agriculture (USDA) deems the meat safe to eat, it may also, at the farmer's request, slap a quality grade on it, too.

Beef: USDA Prime means it's going to make your mouth water. Thanks to the abundant marbling of fat throughout the meat, it'll be tender, juicy, and flavorful. Fire up the grill! USDA Choice is second best. It's a little leaner, which means it won't be quite as juicy as the Prime, but it'll still be mighty fine. USDA Select has much less marbling, which means it'll be less juicy and flavorful. Still, if you have the time to dress it up and marinate it for a good while, you can make it into something decent.

Pork: Pigs are graded on a pass–fail system, and all the fresh cuts in any grocery store are deemed "acceptable." The failed "utility"-grade cuts are only used in processed products and aren't for sale to you.

Chicken: Look for a grade A rating, which means it's of the highest quality. If your butcher is trying to sell you grade B or C, run away. Fast.

Step 3: Choose your cut. The tenderness of the meat largely depends on its location on the animal, and the animal's age. The less-exercised muscles, like those along the back or ribs, will generally be tastier than the frequently used muscles, like the rump, shoulders, and legs. Here's a quick rundown:

Beef: The most tender cuts include filet mignon, tenderloin, T-bone, porterhouse, sirloin, and rib eye, all from the back. You'll need to do very little to these cuts to make them taste good: Add some salt and pepper and cook them over dry heat, which means on the grill, in a good cast-iron skillet, or under the broiler. Flank, skirt, and hanger steak—all from the belly area—do well on the grill, too, especially if you marinate them first. Tougher cuts include rump roasts, brisket, round steaks, shanks, and pot roast. To make them swallowable (and delicious), just cook them with moist heat, which will help break down the tissue and make it more tender. Braise them or toss them in a stew.

Pork: Ham is the heinie of the pig, and you know how good that tastes. Bacon comes from the belly. And almost everything else tender and delicious comes from the loin: tenderloin, chops, cutlets, and baby back ribs.

Chicken: Whoever named whole chickens is kind of awesome because the chicken's name tells you exactly how you should cook it. "Broiler-fryers" are seven- to ten-week-old babes, weighing under 3½ pounds, and you should broil or fry them. "Roasters" are a few weeks older and a few pounds bigger, and, duh, you should roast them. Chicken breasts, which are white meat, are the leanest, most tender cuts of the bird. The fattier dark-meat drumsticks and thighs are cheaper, but you can do great things with them, like fry 'em up.

Step 4: Do your own inspection. Even if you've found a cut of meat with the right grade and at the right price, give it a good once-over to make sure it lives up to what's advertised. Check the sell-by date, look for holes in the packaging, and lastly, examine the meat itself.

Beef: It should be bright red, not gray. If it's sitting in its own juices, that probably means it wasn't stored at the proper temperature, and you should walk on by.

Pork: Look for a grayish-pink color with relatively little fat on the outside. The bones, if there are any, should be lighter in color.

Chicken: Color can vary from bluish white to yellow, and the skin should be cream-colored to yellow.

More Handy Tips

- Meat should never be stinky. If you catch a whiff of something foul, and you know for a fact that it wasn't you or the guy standing next to you, throw the meat away.

- Consider buying meat directly from your local farmer. Some will let you buy a whole, half, or quarter of a cow or pig; if you have the storage space in your freezer, you can ask the farmer or your butcher to cut it and wrap it for you, and you'll be set for a good long while. Too much? Go in on it with your neighbors or friends.

- Freeze your meat, if you don't plan on using it right away. Beef steaks and whole chickens will last a year. Chicken parts will be good for nine months. Pork chops will hang on for four. Ground beef or stew meat is good frozen for three months. Ham is good for two, and bacon for only one. But seriously, who can make bacon last any longer than one weekend?

Get Fired Up

• • •

*"I certainly have learned not to turn my steaks over too much. Turn them
only once. That keeps the juicy juices in."*
—BOB KELLY

HOW TO GRILL A STEAK

Step 1: Buy good meat. Invest in a prime-grade, well-marbled (read:
juicy), 1- to 1½-inch-thick cut, like a rib eye, Porterhouse, T-bone, or
strip steak. Because the steak is going to be the centerpiece of your
meal, don't cheap out. Even if you're a godly grill master, there's not
much you can do with a lousy piece of meat, except marinate the heck
out of it and pray it doesn't taste like your shoe.

Step 2: Grab an ice-cold drink and wave to your neighbor. He's
going to be really jealous really soon.

Step 3: Fire up your grill. If you don't have a chimney starter,
available for a few bucks at any hardware store, go get one now. Then
stuff the bottom with loosely crumpled newspaper, pour charcoal briquettes in the top, remove the cooking grate from the grill, set the
chimney on the bottom grate, and light the paper with a match. When
your briquettes are glowing red and covered in ash, dump them onto
the grate and, using tongs or a shovel, arrange them into a pile that's a
bit higher on one side than the other. Replace the cooking grate, open
the vents on the lid, cover your fire, and let it swelter for about five
minutes.

Step 4: Season your steak. Pat your meat dry with a paper towel, then brush it with olive oil and sprinkle on generous amounts of kosher salt and cracked pepper. A teaspoon per side should do it.

Step 5: Grill it to perfection. Using a pair of tongs, transfer your steak onto the cooking grate above the highest, hottest coals. Wait two minutes until those mouthwatering char lines appear, then rotate it clockwise by a quarter turn. Wait two more minutes, then flip it and re-peat. Unless you want your meat to still be mooing when it's on your plate, let it finish cooking, but over lower heat. Lift it up with your tongs and set it on the grate above a single layer of coals for a few more minutes until it cooks to your desired doneness.

Step 6: Give it a rest. Once your steak is cooked, set it on a clean plate and let it rest for five to ten minutes, so it can get juicy and you can grab another drink before you sit down. Sprinkle with a touch more salt and serve.

More Handy Tips

- Let your steak come to room temperature before seasoning it and setting it on the grill.

- Cooking with lighter fluid may be fun, but it makes your food taste like chemicals. Skip it, if you can.

- Grill grates are easier to clean when they're hot. If yours are crusty from your last meal, scrub them down with a wiry brass brush after you light the grill but before you lay your meat on the grate.

- For goodness' sake, try not to catch anything on fire. Keep your grill at least ten feet away from your house and any trees. If your fire should get out of control, smother it with your kosher salt and shut the lid.

- Use a meat thermometer to test doneness. To be totally safe, you're technically not supposed to eat any steak that hasn't reached an internal temp of 145 degrees. However, if you're willing to risk it for a juicer, more tender steak, then pull it off when it reaches 130 degrees. It'll be a perfectly pink medium rare.

Smoke It

• • •

"We had smokehouses. We smoked everything. We'd bring home six or seven wild turkeys, and we'd skin 'em, clean 'em, and hang 'em in a smokehouse and smoke 'em. That was a staple. For years, drying food was the only way to preserve it. It's still good today!"

—BILL HOLLOMAN

HOW TO MAKE BEEF JERKY

Step 1: Befriend your butcher. Buy 1 to 1½ pounds of lean top round or flank steak, and have him slice it into ¼-inch-thick strips. Or take your meat home, pop it in the freezer for an hour or so until it firms up, and slice it yourself using a sharp knife. Just make sure you cut off any and all fat, which will spoil your jerky.

Step 2: Mix your marinade. In a bowl, stir together 1½ teaspoons of salt, ½ teaspoon of cracked pepper, 2 tablespoons of brown sugar, ¼ cup of soy sauce, 2 tablespoons of Worcestershire sauce, 2 to 4 cloves of crushed garlic, and, if you'd like, a dash of Liquid Smoke.

Step 3: Season your meat. Lay your beef strips in a glass or ceramic dish, pour the marinade over the top, cover, and let sit in your refrigerator for four to six hours—or, even better, overnight. Then the flavor will really soak in.

Step 4: Dry it. Preheat your oven to 140 degrees. While it's warming up, remove your beef from the marinade and pat each piece dry with a paper towel. If you don't have dehydrator trays, lay the slices of beef close together on cake racks, set on cookie trays. (That way air will be able to circulate on all sides of the meat.) Place it in the oven, set your timer for three hours, and check on it then. You'll know your jerky is done when you bend a piece and it cracks, but doesn't break in half. If it's not there yet, let it cook longer. Depending on its thickness, it could take up to ten whole hours or more, so find something to do around the house for a while.

Step 5: Crank it up. Not to be too terribly gross, but this quick step will wipe out any nasty microorganisms that call your meat home. During the final ten minutes of drying, turn your oven up to 275 degrees.

Step 6: Cool and store. Once your jerky is done, pat it dry with a paper towel and let it cool. Then toss it into a glass jar or sealed plastic bags. It'll keep at room temperature for two weeks, longer if you store it in the fridge.

More Handy Tips

- Slice your meat with the grain for chewier jerky, and across the grain for a snappier, more brittle jerky.

- Make up your own marinade. Start with a base of soy sauce, salt, and pepper. After that, add whatever you like to taste. Some ideas: honey, lemon, garlic, brown sugar, Tabasco, whatever looks good to you.

Head the Table

· · ·

"Presentation matters. Make it look good."
—Joe Toth

How to Carve a Roasted Bird

Step 1: Choose your longest, most impressive-looking knife, and hone it. The sharper your blade, the less likely it'll appear that a caveman cooked your Thanksgiving dinner.

Step 2: Position the turkey breast-side up, drumsticks pointing toward you, and snip off any strings.

Step 3: Remove the legs. With your knife along the body, blade down, slice through the skin that attaches the leg to the body, down through the thigh meat, and finally through the joint, where the bones meet. (Don't saw through any bones, Hannibal. You'll make a mess. Just use the tip of your knife to sever the joint.) Set the leg and thigh aside, and repeat once more unless you bought a one-legged bird. (If you did that, hopefully you got a discount.)

Step 4: Poke that crazy-long, two-pronged fork that you've probably never used and that came with your knife set into the wing to secure the bird, and then turn your knife blade parallel to your work surface and make a horizontal cut in the bird, just above the wing and below the breast.

Step 5: Poke your fork into the top of the bird, place your knife halfway up the breast, and slice down until you meet your horizontal cut. Place that piece of meat on a serving platter, and repeat, working your way up the breast to carve thin slices.

More Handy Tips

- Let your bird rest for fifteen to twenty minutes before carving to seal in the juices.

- Sneak a folded paper towel between the turkey and the plate. It'll keep the turkey from sliding around.

- Separate the drumsticks from the thighs before serving to prevent fights at your table.

- Trim off the wings, if anyone would like those, at their joints with poultry shears.

- If you have any questions while carving, and your grandfather isn't around to call, try the Butterball Turkey Hotline at 1–800-BUTTERBALL. Seriously. It's open weekdays from 10 AM to 7 PM (CST), and operators will answer all your birdbrained questions for free.

Live Strong

. . .

"Do everything in your power to feel good and be healthy. Everybody should be striving for that."
—Bob Kelly

HOW TO EAT HEALTHY

Step 1: Know where your food comes from. If it didn't once walk, swim, or grow out of the ground, you probably shouldn't eat so much of it. (And in case you're wondering, no, Twinkies do not grow on trees.) Overdoing it with the highly processed foods, the kind with ingredients you can't even pronounce, can only lead to weight gain or, worse, a ticker that eventually just stops tocking. Opt for real food whenever you can. Reach for a bowl of cherries rather than a cherry-flavored slurpee. Have a few pieces of cheese rather than a handful of Cheetos. You get the point, and soon enough you'll find that the real stuff tastes better anyway, and it keeps you fuller longer, too.

Step 2: Eat when you're hungry. Not when you're bored, anxious, or sad. Food is fuel, not entertainment.

Step 3: Slow down. It takes twenty minutes for the stomach to tell the brain it's full. Avoid overeating (and that sick stuffed feeling that comes with it) by putting your fork down (or at least taking a breath) between bites. Your food isn't going anywhere, so take your time eating it, and stop when you feel satisfied. If you're served much more than you can eat, you're under no obligation to finish everything in front of you, and you don't get a sticker if you do.

More Handy Tips

- Cook for yourself. That way you'll know, and be in control of, exactly what you're eating.

- Eating meat doesn't make you manly, and eating salad doesn't make you womanly. Everybody needs veggies, and lots of them, for a healthy body.

- If you're confused about what's healthy, try dunking your food in water. If it looks pretty much the same, eat it. If it looks like your dog puked it up, don't. Think about it: Underwater carrots? Same. Chicken? Same. Apples? Same. Potato chips? Gross. Fruity Pebbles? Gross. Doritos? Oh, my God, so gross.

Meet Joe

. . .

"I like my coffee navy-style. You put an extra spoonful in. It's a little stronger."
—Al Sulka

How to Make a Good Cup of Coffee

Step 1: Put on your slippers, shuffle out to the kitchen, open your eyes halfway, and gather your supplies: a French press, some high-quality beans (locally roasted, if possible), a grinder, a kettle, a tablespoon, and your favorite mug.

Step 2: Fill your kettle with water, and while you bring it to a boil, go brush your teeth, collect your newspaper, or do whatever else you need to do. Remove the kettle from the heat when it whistles.

Step 3: Grind your beans for a few seconds. That's all it takes for a press pot; otherwise, your coffee will be too fine, and it'll slip through your pot's mesh filter, leaving you with sludge. Your grounds should look like pebbly sand.

Step 4: Measure out your ground coffee and toss it into your press pot. You'll need about one tablespoon for every four ounces of water, more if you want a little hair on your chest.

Step 5: Vigorously pour your hot water (now about 195 to 205 degrees) into your pot. As the steam rises up, breathe it in and think about how much you love coffee. After about a minute of daydreaming, give your pot a stir and then add the lid.

Step 6: Wait three more minutes. Get your milk and sugar ready, if you need them.

Step 7: Press the plunger, pour, beat your chest, and enjoy. Today is going to be a great day!

More Handy Tips

- Store your coffee beans in an airtight container at room temperature away from sunlight.

- No French press? Well, the coffee-to-water ratio is the same no matter what you use to brew. Your grind, however, will change. With an automatic pot, use a medium grind for flat-bottomed filters and a fine grind for cone-shaped ones. Use that same fine grind for stovetop espresso makers. Go extra-fine for an espresso machine.

- Burr grinders work better than blade grinders, which can create uneven grounds and therefore muddy coffee.

- Never reuse your coffee beans. Instead, toss them into your compost pile out back. They'll help things grow.

Pump Iron

. . .

"A cast-iron skillet is an essential in every kitchen. Never wash it in soap and water. Cast iron is porous; it holds soapy water, and you can taste it. No soap, or you'll kill my skillet! I'm the best cook in the world."
—BILL HOLLOMAN

HOW TO SEASON A CAST-IRON SKILLET

Step 1: Look at your skillet admiringly. Give it some love, treat it right, and it'll last you a lifetime.

Step 2: Slick it up. Coat your skillet, inside and out, with vegetable oil or unflavored shortening. Use a paper towel to move the oil around and make sure you get into every nook and cranny. It's going to get slippery, so don't drop it on your toe!

Step 3: Bake it. Place your skillet, upside down, on the top rack in a 350-degree oven for an hour. Place a cookie sheet on the bottom rack, in case any oil drips. When your timer beeps, turn off your oven, leaving the pan inside until it's cool enough to handle.

Step 4: Dry off your skillet, using a clean paper towel. Now it's ready to go. Soon enough, your skillet will become the trustiest, non-stickiest pan in your entire kitchen arsenal.

More Handy Tips

- To clean, just rinse the pan with hot water right away, and then dry it immediately to prevent rust. Skip the soap, unless you like soapy-tasting food.

- If you burn something in your pan, pour coarse salt in it and scrub it with your dish brush. Remember, no soap.

- If your pan begins to rust, scrub it with steel wool and season it again.

- You can season your skillet as often as you like. It helps protect it from rust and creates a natural nonstick surface.

- Final quiz: What should you never wash your skillet with? Hint: It has four letters and rhymes with *dope*.

Give Sweet Rewards

• • •

"We could have ice cream anytime we wanted. We had an icehouse with big ice blocks. We'd take a grain sack out there and chisel a half a block of ice and throw it in the bag. Then we'd lay it on a rock and pound it with a baseball bat until it broke into small pieces. Then we'd get the eggs, the milk, and sugar, and take turns cranking it. During strawberry season, we'd put some of those in, too."

—Philip Spooner

How to Make Ice Cream

Step 1: In a medium bowl, mix 1½ cups of whole milk and ¾ cup of sugar, and whisk until the sugar dissolves. Stir in 1½ cups of heavy cream and 1 tablespoon of vanilla.

Step 2: Add the mixture to your ice cream maker. If you have an electric one, well, fancy you! Check the manufacturer's guidelines to see how much it can hold. Then turn it on, pour the allotted mixture into the frozen bowl, and let it do its work for about half an hour. If you're doing it the old-fashioned way with a hand-crank machine, you'll need to fill the can three-quarters of the way full with your ice cream mixture, set it in the bucket, and then fill the bucket with three parts crushed ice to one part rock salt. Turn the crank for about twenty to thirty minutes, until the ice cream freezes.

Step 3: Let it ripen. Remove the dasher, or paddle, and pop your ice cream in the freezer for an hour or two more before serving.

More Handy Tips

- Once you've got this most basic recipe down, try variations. To make strawberry ice cream, omit the vanilla and add a box of washed, hulled, and crushed fresh strawberries to the mix before freezing. To make a creamier, custard-based ice cream, add eggs. That one's a little more complicated, so do yourself a favor and go find a good ice cream recipe book.

- If you have leftover ice cream mixture, you may store it in the fridge for up to three days. Surely you'll need to make another batch of ice cream by then!

Pour a Draft

• • •

"We made our root beer, or we'd go to the little root beer stand down the street, and for five cents we'd buy it in a cold frosty mug with the foamed-up head in there. Man, that was good!"
—Buck Buchanan

HOW TO MAKE ROOT BEER

Step 1: Gather your ingredients: 1½ teaspoons of root beer extract (available in some grocery stores, wine- and beer-making supply stores, and at various places online, like www.zatarains.com), 1 cup of sugar, ¼ teaspoon of yeast, warm water, and a two-liter bottle. Since the yeast will naturally carbonate your root beer, consider using a plastic bottle rather than a glass one. If you accidentally forget about it and the pressure builds up and it explodes (yes, it could happen), you won't accidentally hurt anyone. Death by root beer would be so tragic.

Step 2: Activate the yeast. Sprinkle your yeast into ½ cup of warm (but not hot!) water. (It should be about the same temp as your armpit—about ninety-eight degrees. Much hotter, and you'll kill your yeast. Use a thermometer to test the temp, or just guess. Don't try to stick your armpit under the water.) Stir, and let dissolve.

Step 3: Add the good stuff. Pop a funnel into the top of your empty bottle and pour in the sugar and root beer extract. Then fill your bottle halfway with warm (but remember, not hot!) water, put the lid on, and shake to dissolve.

Step 4: Add the bubbly stuff. Unscrew the lid, pop in your funnel again, and pour your yeast mixture into the bottle. That's what's going to make it bubbly. Then fill to the neck with warm (but not you-know-what) water, screw the lid on tightly, and shake.

Step 5: Wait. Set your bottle in a dark, room-temperature closet for about three days until it carbonates. If you're using a plastic bottle, give it a squeeze. If it's soft, give it another day. If it's hard, proceed to step 6.

Step 6: Chill. Put your root beer in the fridge until cold, then pour into a frosty mug and gulp it down so fast that you get a foam mustache. That's the only proper way to drink it.

More Handy Tips

• Make a homemade root beer float by adding a scoop of vanilla ice cream (see page 236) to it.

• Make a frosty mug by dunking one in water and then setting it in the freezer until you're ready to use it.

• Home-brewed root beer contains trace amounts of alcohol, but only about one-twelfth the amount in the average beer. That's not enough to worry about for most people, even little ones.

• To make cream soda, replace the root beer extract with vanilla.

- To make ginger ale, skip the root beer extract and add 1½ teaspoons of pureed fresh ginger and the juice of one lemon.

- No yeast handy, or you're frightfully scared of explosions? Boil 1½ cups of water; stir in ¾ cup of sugar and 1½ teaspoons of root beer extract. Refrigerate, and add chilled club soda or seltzer before serving.

11

Hosting

. . .

*Have fun and make other people happy, and good times will
follow you wherever you go.*

Celebrate Good Times

• • •

"For a good party, you've got to have good cocktails. And you've got to make your guests feel like they're at home. Welcome them, treat them well, and make sure they're taken care of."

—BOB KELLY

HOW TO THROW A PARTY

Step 1: Find something to celebrate. Sure, your birthday, your parents' anniversary, your new house, new babe, or new job are all great excuses to plan a get-together, but you hardly need a monumental reason to entertain your friends. After all, what better occasion is there to celebrate than, oh, any old Friday, or Saturday, or National Pie Day? You can basically use anything as an excuse to round up your buds and have a good time.

Step 2: Decide on details. Figure out the date, time, and location of your fête. While you're at it, consider your budget, too.

Step 3: Make your guest list. Depending on the location of the party and your budget, write down all the people you'd like to invite, and then give your list a once-over to make sure you've got a good mix. If you're throwing the party in a small space, you may need to limit the number of people you'll invite, or your guests will just be sweaty and miserable. If you've got a large area to fill, invite lots of folks to avoid awkward empty spaces. Figure about three out of every four people you invite will attend.

Step 4: Invite your peeps. Your guests will get their first impression of your party from the invitation, so make it special. Paper invites, dropped in the mail about three weeks prior to the event, are the most special, but if you don't have the time, or the budget, extend personal invitations via email or telephone to every guest. You want every person to feel important and valued, and mass invites, while convenient for you, just don't do the job.

Step 5: Plan your menu. Make a few grazing stations: meats, cheese and crackers, nuts, olives, chips and salsa. Make a few belly-filling foods, too, since you want your guests to stick around for the fun and not leave early in search of grub. Think protein, like baby meatballs; chilled, boiled shrimp; or anything with bacon. Mmm, bacon. While you're planning your food, figure out what you'd like to serve to drink. Unless it's a child's birthday party, in which case you might have punch or juice, plan on having wine, beer, soda, and one signature cocktail, if not a full bar.

Step 6: Shop. A few days before your party, hit the grocery and liquor stores for all your supplies, including food, drinks, party supplies (plates, silverware, glasses, decorations, candles), and, of course, toilet paper. Start making extra ice, too, if you don't plan on buying it.

Step 7: Clean up. You'll have plenty of business to attend to on the day of the party, so don't leave the dusting, vacuuming, and picking up of dirty socks and undies for last. Do it a few days ahead of time, and then try your darnedest not to mess up your place until the big day.

Step 8: Prep your food. Make anything you can a day or two ahead of time, and pop those dishes in the refrigerator or freezer so you can just warm 'em up on the big night. If your drinks aren't being chilled yet and you have room in the fridge, you might as well tuck them in there as well.

Step 9: Make the finishing touches. On the day of the party, finish any cooking you need to do, set up your bar (don't forget the ice and any garnishes for the drinks), and decorate your house. For classy affairs, nothing beats fresh flowers and tea lights on tabletops to set the mood.

Step 10: Get yourself ready. Take a shower, get dressed, and wait for the guests to arrive. It's your big day. Don't forget to enjoy it!

More Handy Tips

- Music sets the mood of a party faster than anything else. Make your playlist well ahead of time, and consider the cadence of the party as you order your songs. In other words, save "Low" by Flo Rida for well after dark.

- As a host, it's your responsibility to make sure every guest feels welcome. Keep one eyeball on the door, and be sure to personally greet everyone who attends. Keep your other eyeball on anybody standing awkwardly alone. Nobody likes to feel marooned at a party, so take it upon yourself to make everyone feel comfortable and loved.

- Stay in good form. It's fine to have a good time as host, but don't overdo it on the booze. You've got to be sharp enough to take care of your guests. They shouldn't have to take care of you.

- Games can get a party off to a rollicking good start or even save some parties from slow death by boredom. Have a few in your back pocket, like charades, which you can whip out if necessary.

Mix It Up

...

"In the past, I could go out with the best of them. The first time I was in a bar, the bartender asked me, 'What kind of cocktail do you want?' I'd heard somebody say a 7 and 7. I didn't know what it was but it sounded like something good to have. So, I ordered a 7 and 7, and he gave me one. 'I'll have a 7 and 7!' I used to be able to say that with a lot of authority."
—CHUCK TATUM

HOW TO TEND BAR

Step 1: Stock your bar. With a few pieces of basic equipment, you'll be able to mix just about any drink. Make sure you have: a bottle opener, an ice bucket and tongs, a cocktail shaker, a jigger, a long spoon, a muddler, a paring knife, and plenty of glasses.

Step 2: Buy the good stuff. Any drink is only as good as the ingredients you put in it, so invest in decent liquor, especially if you plan on serving it neat, and always have plenty of real fruit on hand that you can use to either garnish your cocktails or make fresh juice. The difference between using freshly squeezed lemon juice and that stuff that comes in a plastic yellow lemon is immeasurable. Let's just say both drinks will blow minds, but only one will do it in a good way.

Step 3: Follow the recipe. Be precise with your measurements. Use a jigger, if you must, or practice pouring on your own until you can accurately eyeball your ounces. Also, shake or stir only as prescribed, or you risk clouding good liquor. As a rule of thumb, stir clear drinks and anything with bubbles. Shake cloudy drinks, which is usually anything mixed with fruit juice, cream, or sugar.

Step 4: Memorize a few classic cocktails. While most people will order highballs, like gin and tonics or 7 and 7s (which is Seagram's 7 whiskey and 7UP), it's essential that you have a few decent drinks in your repertoire.

An Old-Fashioned: Drop a sugar cube (or ½ teaspoon of sugar) in a heavy-bottomed, short tumbler. Add three dashes of Angostura bitters, and crush them together with a wooden muddler. Whirl your glass around so the sugar coats the inside. Add an ice cube, followed by 1½ ounces of bourbon. Add a lemon twist or—if you want to get super-fancy—a skewered cherry, orange slice, and pineapple chunk.

A Sidecar: Pour three-quarter ounce of brandy, three-quarter ounce of Cointreau, and three-quarter ounce of fresh lemon juice into an ice-filled cocktail shaker and shake. Wet the rim of a stemmed cocktail glass and roll it on a small sugar-coated plate. Strain the liquor into the sugar-rimmed glass.

A Daiquiri: Over an ice-filled shaker, squeeze the juice from half a lime. Add a teaspoon of powdered sugar and 1½ ounces of light rum. Shake vigorously, and strain into a stemmed cocktail glass.

A Gimlet: Mix three ounces of gin with one ounce of Rose's lime juice in an ice-filled cocktail shaker. Shake, and strain into a cocktail glass. (For a vodka gimlet, replace the gin with vodka.)

More Handy Tips

- Be generous with the ice, and always add your liquor to the cubes, not the other way around.

- Chill your glasses. After your guest orders a drink, fill the appropriate glass with ice and water (or just crushed ice) so it can chill while you mix the cocktail. Cold drinks should only be served in cold glasses.

- Serve all drinks with a cocktail napkin.

- If you want to taste the cocktail before handing it to your guest, don't sneak a slurp. Instead, dip a straw into the shaker, put your finger over one end, and then release it into your mouth. Just don't double-dip!

Clink Glasses

• • •

"If you have a dinner party, make a toast. Have a message. Here's to a successful marriage, a successful new birth, a successful graduation. You give a toast because you're wishing something for the person you're toasting. A toast is a recognition."
—BILL HOLLOMAN

HOW TO MAKE A TOAST

Step 1: Get your guests' attention. If the room is large and loud, stand up at your table and gently tap your spoon against your glass. Those around you will soon join in until the room quiets down.

Step 2: Take a deep breath. All eyes are on you, and since you called this attention to yourself, expectations will surely be high. Pray that your fly is zipped, and then relish the moment.

Step 3: Make your speech. Introduce yourself, if not everyone knows you. Give thanks to your guest or guests for joining you in this celebration, if you're the host. And then either share a short, sweet, or funny anecdote that relates to the cause of the celebration or cut straight to it and simply share your good wishes.

Step 4: Raise your glass, and invite your guests to raise theirs with you. Then make a sincere, heartfelt wish for the person or people you're toasting. You can never go wrong with, "Here's to a wonderful _____!"

More Handy Tips

- Keep your drinking to a minimum until after you deliver your speech. Giving a drunken toast is not only embarrassing for you, but also annoying for your guests.

- Know what you're going to say before you make your toast. It's a celebration, not improv night at the comedy club.

- Toasts can be fun—and funny—but if you learned yours on spring break or it begins with, "There once was a girl from Nantucket," save it for another time.

Come Again

...

"You get invited back if you make the hosts feel like the best hosts around. They want to be successful and they want you to have a good time and think, Wow, I'd like to do it again! *If you treat them that way, you'll be invited back."*

—Frank Walter

How to Be a Gracious Guest

Step 1: Show up when you're welcome. That means if a friend invites you over for dinner at 7 PM, arrive at 7 PM, no sooner, no later. Or if you're visiting friends or family out of town, even if you know you have an open invitation to crash, call ahead of time to make sure it's still all right.

Step 2: Come bearing gifts. It doesn't have to be anything major, but a bouquet of flowers, a bottle of wine, a pound of locally roasted coffee, or something special from home will always start the visit off right.

Step 3: Chip in. Don't confuse being a guest with being a king, who expects to be waited upon at every turn. Get up off your duff and help out whenever possible. Offer to set the table, wash some dishes, or chip in with any necessary work that needs to be done. Oftentimes, your host will insist you relax, at which point do so, but only after you've volunteered your services.

Step 4: Say thanks. Show your host your gratitude twice: Do it when you're leaving and then be sure to send a thank-you card once you've gone. Follow these rules, and you'll always be invited back.

More Handy Tips

- Know when it's time to go. If the host start to yawn, turns on the lights, gets into his or her pajamas, or says, "Wow, it's so late," that's your cue that you've already overstayed your welcome. Say thanks, grab your coat, and hightail it out of there.

- If you've stayed overnight, always strip your bed and toss your dirty sheets and dirty towels in the hamper.

- If your hosts tells you to make yourself at home, that doesn't mean you should eat every last bit of ice cream in the freezer or walk around in your underwear. And for goodness' sake, don't ever do both at once!

Get Laughs

...

"Tell a lot of jokes, and make people laugh. Tell jokes with double entendres. They're subtle, so you're always safe."
—ANGEL RODRIGUEZ

HOW TO TELL A CLEAN JOKE

Step 1: Memorize your joke. In fact, write it down and practice it a few times out loud, so you can master not only the words, but also your comic timing. You'll get the hook if you start a joke and forget the details or the punch line. Get your material down pat before you take it out on the road. You can't go wrong with this classic: "Did you hear about the man who went to the doctor with a carrot up his nose? The doctor says, 'I know exactly what's wrong with you. You're not eating properly!'"

Step 2: Know your audience. It doesn't matter if *you* think a joke is funny. Your audience has got to think it's funny, too. To be safe, stay away from anything offensive, which includes jokes about religion, gender, race, sexual orientation, or your pal's sweetie or mama.

Step 3: Deliver it. Once you start a joke, you've got to finish it. There's no turning back. Keep a straight face, look your audience in the eye, and let 'er rip.

More Handy Tips

- Unless you're hanging out with Bob Saget, never repeat an offensive joke, especially if the punch line is, "The aristocrats!"

- Only do an accent if you're good at it. How to tell? Quick, say, "How to build a fire" in Scottish. Now, try Irish. Then, Australian. Finally, British. Do they all sound exactly the same, Indian or southern? Then no accents for you!

- Nobody laughed at your joke? Don't sweat it. They probably won't remember your joke anyway. They'll just remember that you tried to brighten their day.

Blow Hard

. . .

"I've worn out dozens of harmonicas! I used to play once a month at a barn dance. An old lady would play the piano, an old fella would play the violin, his wife would play the drums, and I'd play harmonica. At some point, I'd even play a solo. The small ones make better music."

—Philip Spooner

HOW TO PLAY THE HARMONICA

Step 1: Cup the harmonica. Most harmonicas have numbered holes, 1 through 10, with 1 being the lowest note and 10 being the highest. Hold the harmonica parallel to the ground so the numbers are on top and read 1 to 10, left to right. (If your harmonica doesn't have numbers, make sure the low notes are on your left.) Now, using either hand, pinch the pads of your forefinger and thumb together, then open gently and slide your harmonica between them until it's snug against the webbing on your hand. That's it! If you want to create a vibrato sound with your harmonica, loosely curl the middle, ring, and pinkie fingers of your harmonica-holding hand behind the instrument to create a megaphone effect. Then use your opposite hand, palm facing up, to cup your first hand and create an airtight seal behind the harmonica. Wiggle that hand, if you want to get fancy.

Step 2: Pucker up. Stand in front of the mirror and push your lips out as far from your face as you can without pursing them. If you look like a goldfish, then you're doing it right. Next, place your harmonica inside, not on, your puckered lips, and try to blow through a single hole to get a single note. Keep practicing and adjusting your mouth until you get the seal right.

Step 3: Breathe. Depending on whether you blow (exhale) or draw (inhale), you'll hear a different note. Regardless of the direction of the air, you should always breathe from your diaphragm, not your throat or chest. Place one hand on your belly and practice playing one note, blowing and drawing. If your hand moves, you'll know that you're breathing correctly.

Step 4: Practice. And then practice some more. And after that, guess what you need to do? Yep, practice a little longer. It takes a while to become a master, but you'll get there in time. Here's a song to get you started. The numbers correspond to the holes, and a minus (-) sign before a number means draw. Otherwise, blow.

Home on the Range

6   6   7 -8 8
Oh, give me a home

7   -7 -6 -9 -9   -9
where the buf-fa-lo roam,

8 -9   9
And the deer

7   7   7   -7   7   -8
and the an-te-lope play.

6   6   7 -8   8
Where sel-dom is heard

7 -7   -6 -9 -9   -9
a dis-cour-a-ging word,

-9 -9   8
And the sky

-8 7   -7   7 -8 7
is not cloud-y all day.

9   -9   8 -8   8
Home, home on the range.

More Handy Tips

- To bend your notes (or get all bluesy and slide them down by a half or whole step), you've got to actually change the air pressure in your mouth. It takes practice, so be patient. On holes 1 through 6, inhale and quickly drop your tongue into the bottom of your mouth as if you were saying "ee-oh." On holes 7 through 10, exhale and do the same thing.

- Harmonicas go by many names. They're also called Blues Harps, Blues Burgers, Mississippi Saxophones, Tin Biscuits, Toot Sweets, Fist Whistles, and Lickin' Sticks. Feel free to call yours whatever you like, even, um, Monica.

- For free harmonica tabs, visit www.harptabs.com.

Puff Up

• • •

"Part of smoking a pipe is relighting it. While you're thinking of an answer you're going to give to someone else, light that pipe, take a couple of puffs, and then give your answer. That makes you look smart."
—BUCK BUCHANAN

HOW TO SMOKE A PIPE

Step 1: Choose your pipe. They range in price from a few bucks to a few thousand bucks, but the right pipe for you is simply one you love, whether it's made of corncob, wood (usually briar), a calabash gourd, or meerschaum, which looks like white soapstone. Just hold a few different types in your hand and see which one feels best.

Step 2: Pack it. Take each pinch of fresh tobacco and gently roll it between your fingers to check the moisture content. (If it's too wet-feeling, set your pinch on a napkin or in a bowl and let it dry out for a while while you make yourself an Old-Fashioned; see page 247.) Then add your tobacco to your pipe in three passes. First, sprinkle it in the bowl, level off the top, and, using a tamper, gently press it down so it only fills about a third of the bowl. Repeat: Sprinkle, level, and tamp so the tobacco now fills two-thirds of the bowl. Repeat one last time: Sprinkle, level, tamp so the tobacco is springy and even with the bowl. Now take a test draw. If you feel air swooshing into your mouth, it's correctly packed. If it feels like you're sucking a thick milk shake through a tiny straw, it's packed too tightly; dump your tobacco and try again. Your goal: looser tobacco on the bottom, firmer tobacco on top.

Step 3: Light it. Just as it took three passes to pack your pipe, it'll take you three passes to light it, too. Place your pipe in your mouth, strike a wooden match, and pass the flame around and around over your tobacco as you take several short puffs. You'll notice your tobacco expand and unravel. This is called a false or charring light, and it'll help your tobacco burn evenly. Allow the fire to go out, and very gently tamp down your tobacco until it's again even with the bowl. Repeat once more.

Step 4: Puff it. Light your pipe once more, extinguish your match, take a draw, sit back, and enjoy the flavor. Pipe smoke is meant to be sipped and savored, not swallowed, so do not inhale. Keep your matches handy, and relight it as necessary.

More Handy Tips

- Pipe cleaners aren't just for crafts. They're actually made to clean pipes. Run one through yours between each smoke.

- To keep a briar pipe shiny, rub it alongside your nose while the pipe is still warm. Sounds weird, but the oil in your skin will help give it a nice finish.

- If your pipe keeps going out, you've probably packed it too tightly. Ease up next time.

- Always let the sulfurous tip of the match burn off before putting the flame to your tobacco.

- If the smoke burns your mouth, you're sucking too fast. Go easy.

- Pipe smoking may make you look smart, but it doesn't actually make you smart. It can cause cancer, duh. If you do decide to do it, do it only in moderation.

Spot It

· · ·

"You have to be very bright to play dominoes. I was a domino champion. It's a good way to pass the time without getting into trouble."
—Angel Rodriguez

How to Play Draw Dominoes

Step 1: Shuffle the bones. Using a set that goes up to double-sixes (six dots, or pips, on each side), lay your dominoes facedown on a table and mix them up. Then select your hand, keeping it hidden from the other players. With two players, each person chooses seven dominoes. With three or four players, each chooses five dominoes. The unchosen dominoes remain facedown on the table in what is known as the bone-yard. Mwah-ha-ha!

Step 2: Play the game. The person with the highest double, say double-sixes, lays down that domino first, and play proceeds clock-wise. The next player must lay down a domino with at least one matching number on it. In this case, let's say he plays a six–two, or a domino with six pips on one side and two on the other. Position this domino so it's perpendicular to the double-six, and the six-end is touching the double-six and the two-end is sticking out. If the second player doesn't have a matching domino, he must draw from the bone-yard until he finds and plays one. The next player may now play off *either* open end of the two dominoes. In this case, he may play off the other side of the double-six or the two-end of the six–two. If he plays off the two-end, let's say with a two–three (two pips on one side, three on the other), he should lay it down end-to-end with the six–two so the twos match up. If he plays a double-two, he should lay it down perpendicular to the six–two.

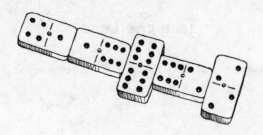

Step 3: Win the round. The round ends when one player plays all his dominoes or play is blocked and no player can go.

Step 4: Score the round. Each pip is worth a point, so at the end of the round, each player should count the number of pips in his hand. The player with the fewest pips, or points, wins the round. His score for the round is the sum of all the other players' hands, minus any points in his own. The game is usually played to one hundred points.

More Handy Tips

- If you don't have a matching domino and the boneyard is empty, play passes over you.

- When you play your last domino, call "Domino!" to end the game.

- Play your doubles whenever you can. Doing so cuts down on your opponent's options.

- If it's that kind of game, and you're having fun, slam your dominoes on the table to faux-intimidate your opponent.

Take the Lead

...

"If you make a mistake when you dance, who cares? Feel free. Float!"
—JOE TOTH

HOW TO GENTLY GUIDE YOUR DANCE PARTNER (WITHOUT SAYING A WORD)

Step 1: Lead with your body. Be strong, but gentle, and communicate your intention to your partner by shifting your entire frame, not just your hands or, worse, your big eyeballs. Never shove or yank your partner around the dance floor, or you'll be dancing alone very soon.

Step 2: Know some moves. If you don't know how to move on the dance floor, how do you expect to lead someone else? Have a few basic steps in your back pocket, and know at least a few beats ahead of time what you'd like to do next.

Step 3: Make her look good. Your ultimate goal is to show your dance partner a good time, and that will happen if she feels happy and swept up in the music. Don't make dancing with you a test or a teaching moment. If she's a beginner, stick with simple steps, allowing her to feel confident and graceful in your arms. If you do that, you'll surely get a second dance.

More Handy Tips

- Keep your eyes open and lead your partner into empty space on the dance floor. If she gets an elbow to the ribs or someone else crashes into her, that's on you, buddy. You're driving.

- Never correct your partner on the dance floor, unless she asks for pointers.

- Look your dance partner in the eyes and smile. If you're knitting your brows, you're concentrating too hard on the moves and not enough on your partner.

- Before you ask anyone to dance, check your breath and your pits. Nobody wants to be twirled by a stinker, even if you've got moves.

- Try to move to the beat, if at all possible, and pay attention to how she's moving, too. Her hips won't lie. If, by the end of the song, she's in your arms, smiling, ask her for another spin. The night is still young, and you're off to a great start.

Acknowledgments

· · ·

I had so much help writing this book, so here is a huge, heartfelt thank-you:

To all of the wonderful grandfathers who shared their stories and wisdom with me. Especially Joe Babin of Cleveland, Ohio, who taught me what it takes to support a family; Buck Buchanan, who always remembers what's important; Bill Holloman, who regaled me with tales of his amazing adventures; Bob Kelly, who reminded me to always follow my dreams; Angel Rodriguez, who welcomed me into his home and served me delicious Cuban pastries; Philip Spooner, who taught me how important it is to stand up for what you believe in; Al Sulka, who gave me so many belly laughs; Chuck Tatum, who taught me what it really means to be brave; Joe Toth, who showed me his drawn-to-scale dollhouse plans over tea and brownies with his family; and Frank Walter, who reminded me that if you're lucky enough to find true love, do whatever you can to hang on to it. I feel honored to know each of you.

To my editors, Kerri Buckley and Jill Schwartzman, for your kindness, support, enthusiasm, and expert eyes; and all my friends at Random House, including Jane von Mehren, Melissa Possick, Leigh Marchant, Theresa Zoro, Katie Rudkin, Tom Nevins, Stacy Berenbaum, and Rebecca Shapiro. Thank you for taking this small idea and helping me make it big.

To all of the modern-day experts who offered their guidance on some of the more technical tips, including: mountain man Brody Henderson, general manager and guide at Alpine River Outfitters in Vail, Colorado; Gennaro Brooks-Church, director of Eco Brooklyn, a green contracting outfit in New York; car whisperer John Huff, service manager at Dave Hallman Hyundai in Erie, Pennsylvania; Jeffrey Klein, director of the Graduate Leadership Program and Wharton Leadership Ventures at the University of Pennsylvania in Philadelphia; money whiz Jonathan F. Walsh, a certified public accountant in New York City; Joe Marchesi, co-founder of Truman's Gentlemen's Groomers in New York City; Sam Buffa, co-owner of F.S.C. Barber in New York City; dog behavior counselor Rikke Brogaard, owner of Rikke Brogaard's Positive Dog Training in Brooklyn; Karen Keough-Huff, athletic director of Amherst Regional High School in Amherst, Massachusetts; Jim Morgans, head football coach at Parkland High School in Orefield, Pennsylvania; Sara Reid Land, former all-county diver and diving coach in North East, Pennsylvania; dandy and shopkeeper Charles Henry of the FineAndDandyShop.com; Sheila C. Ribordy, Ph.D., professor of psychology at DePaul University in Chicago; Nicole Brier, a personal chef in Brooklyn; Aaron Sigmond of Nat Sherman, a tobacconist in New York City; and Lauren Purcell, co-author of *Cocktail Parties, Straight Up!*

To Aunt Kathy, who gave me my first professional writing assignment in her local paper. Before I even had a clue about anything, you gave me a shot, and I'll never forget it.

To my parents, Bill and Claire, for lovingly cheering me on in all that I do, and my in-laws, Norm and Shirley, for teaching me how to build the best driftwood fires on the beach.

To Holly Bemiss, my literary agent and my everything else. Thank you for always inspiring me, championing me, and helping me discover the adventure in every new day.

ABOUT THE AUTHOR

ERIN BRIED is a senior staff writer at *SELF* magazine and the author of *How to Sew a Button: And Other Nifty Things Your Grandmother Knew*. She lives with her better half in Brooklyn, New York, where she plays dominoes, wields power tools, and eats homemade ice cream as often as possible.

ABOUT THE TYPE

The text of this book was set in Janson, a misnamed typeface designed in about 1690 by Nicholas Kis, a Hungarian living in Amsterdam. In 1919 the matrices became the property of the Stempel Foundry in Frankfurt. It is an old-style book face of excellent clarity and sharpness. Janson serifs are concave and splayed; the contrast between thick and thin strokes is marked.